DIGITAL PLAY IN EARLY CHILDHOOD

Sara Miller McCune founded SAGE Publishing in 1965 to support the dissemination of usable knowledge and educate a global community. SAGE publishes more than 1000 journals and over 800 new books each year, spanning a wide range of subject areas. Our growing selection of library products includes archives, data, case studies and video. SAGE remains majority owned by our founder and after her lifetime will become owned by a charitable trust that secures the company's continued independence.

Los Angeles | London | New Delhi | Singapore | Washington DC | Melbourne

MONA SAKR
DIGITAL PLAY IN EARLY CHILDHOOD

What's the problem?

Los Angeles | London | New Delhi
Singapore | Washington DC | Melbourne

Los Angeles | London | New Delhi
Singapore | Washington DC | Melbourne

SAGE Publications Ltd
1 Oliver's Yard
55 City Road
London EC1Y 1SP

SAGE Publications Inc.
2455 Teller Road
Thousand Oaks, California 91320

SAGE Publications India Pvt Ltd
B 1/I 1 Mohan Cooperative Industrial Area
Mathura Road
New Delhi 110 044

SAGE Publications Asia-Pacific Pte Ltd
3 Church Street
#10-04 Samsung Hub
Singapore 049483

Editor: Delayna Spencer
Editorial assistant: Orsod Malik
Production editor: Nicola Carrier
Copyeditor: Chris Bitten
Proofreader: Leigh C. Smithson
Indexer: Gary Kirby
Marketing manager: Dilhara Attygalle
Cover design: Wendy Scott
Typeset by: C&M Digitals (P) Ltd, Chennai, India
Printed in the UK

© Mona Sakr 2020

First published 2020

Apart from any fair dealing for the purposes of research or private study, or criticism or review, as permitted under the Copyright, Designs and Patents Act, 1988, this publication may be reproduced, stored or transmitted in any form, or by any means, only with the prior permission in writing of the publishers, or in the case of reprographic reproduction, in accordance with the terms of licences issued by the Copyright Licensing Agency. Enquiries concerning reproduction outside those terms should be sent to the publishers.

Library of Congress Control Number: 2019937017

British Library Cataloguing in Publication data

A catalogue record for this book is available from the British Library

ISBN 978-1-5264-7457-5
ISBN 978-1-5264-7456-8 (pbk)

At SAGE we take sustainability seriously. Most of our products are printed in the UK using responsibly sourced papers and boards. When we print overseas we ensure sustainable papers are used as measured by the PREPS grading system. We undertake an annual audit to monitor our sustainability.

CONTENTS

About the Author — viii
Acknowledgements — ix

1 Introduction — 1
   Digital play in the everyday life of young children — 1
   Asking open questions about digital play — 1
   A bit about me — 3
   My motivations for writing this book — 4
   Good reasons for reading this book — 6
   How to get the most out of your reading — 6
   Overview of chapters — 9

2 Digital Technologies and Social Interaction — 12
   Introduction — 12
   Digital technologies in a sociocultural context — 14
   How is collaborative creativity in play mediated by digital technologies? — 19
   How is affective alignment mediated by digital technologies? — 25
   Connectedness versus connection — 27
   Further reading — 32

3 Physical Engagement and Sensory Experience in Digital Play — 34
   Introduction — 34
   Active digital play — 35
   Intangibility or a different kind of touch? — 39
   Messy digital play — 44
   Further reading — 49

4 Digital Technologies and Outdoor Play 50

Introduction 50
Are digital technologies to blame for the decline in outdoor play? 51
Technology has always been a part of nature play 55
Social and material constraints around play outdoors with digital technologies 59
Your impressions of digital play in an outdoor environment 60
Further reading 64

5 Imagination and Creativity in Digital Environments 66

Introduction 66
Possibility thinking in digital play 68
Ready-made or remix? 73
Transgressive digital play 77
Further reading 81

6 Digital Play and Media Literacy 83

Introduction 83
Digital media and kinderculture 84
The latest kinderculture craze: 'Baby shark' 85
Digital play and the commercialisation of childhood 88
Parental mediation and media literacy 91
Further reading 95

7 Managing Attention in Digital Environments 97

Introduction 97
Allocating attention in digital play environments 98
Scattered attention in a family environment 100
Fast-paced digital play and attention deficit disorder: Is there a link? 103
Slowing down digital play: What the independent games industry offers 106
Further reading 110

8 Digital Play and a Child's Sense of Self 111

Introduction 111
The Self in relation to others 113
Self-presentation 115
Self-representation 118
Selfies: Self-presentation or self-representation? 119
Further reading 123

9 Digital Play in Context   125
   Introduction   125
   Mediating digital play   126
   Challenging popular discourses surrounding children's digital play   130
   Blurring the boundaries   134
   Further reading   138

10 Conclusion   140
   Shaping the future of digital play in early childhood   140
   Digital play: A debate of many layers   141
   Possibility thinking around digital play: Moving beyond popular
      discourses   144
   Developing a 'guerrilla design' approach to digital play   145
   What children need from us   147
   So what next?   149

References   151
Index   162

ABOUT THE AUTHOR

Dr Mona Sakr is a Senior Lecturer in Education and Early Childhood at Middlesex University. Her research explores play and creativity in early childhood education with a particular interest in how digital technologies are changing the way that children play and create.

ACKNOWLEDGEMENTS

This book involves close observation of children engaging in digital play in a range of settings, including nurseries, schools and the family home. The book therefore wouldn't have been possible without the kind participation of the children, their parents and caregivers, and in some cases, their teachers in the research from which these observations arose. So my first set of thanks must be given to all of the children who feature in the book and all of the adults who have enabled these children to participate in the research. Thank you so much for making this book possible!

I am grateful to all my students at Middlesex University. Your interest in children's digital play – and your willingness to grapple with the implications of contemporary society for children's everyday lives – is the main inspiration underpinning this book. As I wrote the book, my students were constantly in my mind and my greatest hope is that the book feels relevant, interesting and accessible to them.

I also want to express my gratitude to my colleagues at Middlesex University, particularly those in the Education Department, and within this, all the staff teaching on BA Early Childhood Studies and BA Education Studies. I am so incredibly lucky to be part of such a supportive and all-round lovely team! I am in awe of the expertise and dedication of those surrounding me in a professional context, and it is a pleasure to write a book such as this amidst such a wonderful group of individuals.

Finally, I am – as always – indebted to my family and wish to express that here. I am indebted to my parents' encouragement, my husband Tom's unwavering support and the brilliance of our children Leyla and Ishmael (who turn up every so often among the pages of this book).

1
INTRODUCTION

DIGITAL PLAY IN THE EVERYDAY LIFE OF YOUNG CHILDREN

" A 3-year-old girl and her 18-month-old brother are playing games through the 'Sarah and Duck' app on their mother's phone while she tidies up around them. 'Sarah and Duck' is a programme, produced by the BBC, that they love to watch on television, and they are excited about interacting with the characters from the show through the app on the phone. The app involves a sequence of games: from playing virtual snap, to 'tidying up' Sarah's toys on screen by dragging them to the right place, and brushing the characters' teeth through the movement of the finger on the screen. The 3 year old is concentrating and perseveres with each game, even though she is relatively inexperienced with the touch screen and finds the 'drag and drop' motion quite difficult. She is frowning and hunched over, looking at the screen with intensity and not engaging with those around her. Her younger brother is excited about seeing the characters, especially 'Duck'. He points at the phone repeatedly, smiling widely and making eye contact with his mother, and says 'duck' and 'quack' many times. Sometimes he jabs at the phone and his sister gets frustrated that he is getting in the way and 'ruining the game'. "

ASKING OPEN QUESTIONS ABOUT DIGITAL PLAY

Even though this observation is simple – just a few minutes' worth of observation of a common form of everyday digital play – there is a lot going on here.

An observation like this stimulates many questions about young children's learning, development, social interaction, imagination, physical activity, creativity and so much more. We can see an observation like this in different ways. We might feel concern about the 3 year old's experience; we might read her furrowed brow and the way she pushes her younger brother away from the screen as evidence of an unhealthy fixation on the screen – a fixation that hinders her social development. On the other hand, we might see this activity as a fundamental part of the children's developing interests and passions, enabling them to apply their knowledge about the world; after all, the 18 month old seems to be mostly experiencing excitement about his recognition of the duck character on screen. Through his pointing and facial expressions he is using the digital play as a way of connecting with others. We might see the mother's apparent lack of involvement (though the app is on her phone) as an opportunity for independent learning, or we might feel that it is a missed opportunity to mediate the digital play experience for one or both of the children.

A few minutes of observing digital play can lead to lots of questions, and it is often the case that these questions will come loaded with judgements rather than being genuinely open questions. This is because the issue of children's digital play tends to be a forum for intensive and often harsh judgement and typically one in which children's lives are deemed to be 'problematic'. When you read the observation above, what impressions and judgements do you form immediately? If some of your evaluation of the situation was negative (e.g. the children are too passive, they should not be left alone, the screen will damage their eyes, the screen is getting in the way of meaningful interaction, 'this is not real play'), then this is not that surprising given the popular media discourses that surround children's digital play. Most media headlines relate to this judgement: children are losing out, for all sorts of reasons, through their digital play. You can see this for yourself now if you search online for recent news stories about children's digital engagement; you will probably find that of the top five headlines, the majority of these relate to a sense of concern and the idea that contemporary children's engagement in digital play constitutes a 'problem'.

These concerns are of course important. We need to address the potentially negative issues that surround digital play, and this book aims to do this. But it also aims to organise itself around more open questions about children's digital play that are less overwhelmed by judgement. By asking open questions, we can respond to the concerns that surround digital play but also explore the opportunities that emerge through children's digital play. This book aims to model a genuine spirit of open inquiry around the timely issue of digital play in early childhood. The book is also an invitation to explore together through research and theory, but also through our personal and professional observations, reflections and experiences.

This introductory chapter will first explain who I am and my motivations for writing this book; it will then suggest why you might read this book and offer some guidance about how to get the most from the experience. Finally, you will find some brief chapter overviews so that if you are interested in particular aspects of digital play (e.g. imagination, social interaction, physical activity or more), then you will know where to find what is most relevant to you.

A BIT ABOUT ME

I currently teach as a Senior Lecturer at Middlesex University in London on two undergraduate degree programmes: Education Studies and Early Childhood Studies. In this role, I lead two optional modules – one about children's play, and the other about children's creativity. A key aspect of these modules stems from how children's digital engagement is changing the way that children play and enact their creativity. Over the years, I have seen my students trying to make sense of what happens to play and creativity when digital technologies become a fundamental part of children's everyday experiences. I have seen my students struggle with the questions 'Does digital play count as real play?' and 'Can children be as creative when they are engaging in digital environments?'. I have also seen the extent to which popular media headlines about children's digital engagement have influenced how my students see these issues. When we look at digital play, or children's creativity in digital environments, I have been surprised that most of my students have an underlying assumption that digital technologies must be bad for children. They believe this even though they themselves are constantly engaging with their own digital technologies – most often their smartphone. I try to help my students to see that we need to see children's digital play through a more open-minded lens, and that we need to ask genuine questions about what is going on rather than jumping to conclusions about the worth (or lack of worth) of digital play in children's lives. In that respect, this book is a continuation of my teaching.

As well as teaching about digital play, my research over the last 8 years has focused on understanding more about what is going on when children engage in digital play. I have conducted research in nurseries, schools and homes, observing children as they engage with digital technologies. I have analysed these observations looking for different aspects of behaviour and interaction including 1) the emotional dynamics of a situation and how they are influenced by the flow of digital play, 2) opportunities for creativity and collaborative creativity within different digital play environments and 3) how the activity of play moves between different spaces – between the digital environment but also around different elements of the physical environment. Overall, these research projects, alongside a growing body of research conducted by an international range of researchers, have demonstrated that while digital play has some distinct properties, children can essentially still be playful and creative in the context of digital environments. What the research suggests in no way corresponds to the panic and anxiety that is conveyed through media headlines about children's digital engagement. So as researchers, students and practitioners in early childhood, we have a duty to take a step back from the popular discourses that surround children's digital play and look afresh at what is going on and what it means for children's learning and wellbeing.

A final thing I would like to mention here is that I am also a mother to two small children. On the most personal level, I am involved in the debates around children's digital play. I often wonder about which digital technologies to have in the house, which to make available to the children, when to make them available, and how to mediate and monitor what is going on in their digital engagement. You might have guessed that the observation at the start of this chapter actually relates to my own two children. The phone they are playing with in the observation is my phone. All the many questions that arise around the observation are my questions as a mother too: Should the children be playing with this app? Is there something better they could be doing with their time? How should I manage the interaction between the children as they are playing on the app, particularly when they are each engaging with the app in such a distinct way? Should the app just be for the 3 year old, even though the 18 month old seems to be enjoying it so much? Was I right to leave them to play with the app, or should I have been more involved? Did they end up playing with the app for too long, or for not long enough? What did they learn through their engagement with the app? What if they did not learn anything, and just found it fun – is this still a meaningful experience? These are just some of the questions that I have around this kind of experience.

Given that you are probably a student or practitioner in early childhood, and/or perhaps you are a parent yourself, I am sure that the issues around digital play that this book discusses are personal to you too. I am not asking you to leave your own experiences, observations and reflections at the door. As explained more in the following sections, your own personal take on what is going on is an essential part of the dialogue around children's digital play. Your thoughts and opinions, coupled with critical questioning, are a fundamental part of the project represented by this book.

MY MOTIVATIONS FOR WRITING THIS BOOK

As evident in the section above, my motivations for writing this book relate to both my professional and personal involvement in early childhood education and care. In both spheres of experience, the last 10 years have seen a whirlwind of excitement and controversy – fuelled by popular media – about children's digital engagement and the significance of their digital play as part of their everyday lives. For most of the students and practitioners who I work with, the response to this whirlwind has predominantly been one of confusion. They are unsure how to respond. Should they embrace the growth of digital play as a core part of children's lives, and build in more time for this when being with young children, or should they impose some kind of 'digital detox' in order to safeguard children from the excesses of contemporary culture?

Often when I see practitioners and students engaging with the issues, they take up one extreme position or the other so that either they are 'in favour' of digital play or they are 'against' digital play. But positioning the debate in terms of these two extreme positions is perhaps not so helpful and might be adding to our confusion about what to do as part of our everyday lives. I am convinced that a more helpful position to adopt is one great big step back! Rather than trying to find one definitive answer to the 'problem', perhaps we need instead to be prepared to watch and listen intently and ponder what is going on when children engage in digital play. Only then can we become more aware of the myriad opportunities and concerns that are folded into their experiences of digital play.

As individuals working in the early childhood education sector, we are normally experts in observation. Watching, listening and feeling intently is what we are good at, and that is what we can contribute when it comes to making sense of digital play. I wanted to write a book that represents and models this approach in action – prioritising observation and reflection over judgement. At the same time, I did not want to skirt around the issues that concern people the most. It is important to recognise that so many adults in our society do see digital play as a problem, and for all different sorts of reasons, and we need to engage with these popular perceptions and discourses rather than dismissing them. This explains the book's subtitle: 'What's the problem?' The book engages with the different 'problems' that are presented in relation to digital play in early childhood. In fact, each chapter centres on a particular type of 'problem' that digital play in early childhood is often taken to constitute, whether this is physical activity/inactivity, or declining rates of outdoor play and the blame that has been heaped on digital play in relation to this decline. However, each chapter then goes on to unpick the evidence and theoretical perspectives that help us to consider that 'problem' perspective with more criticality and apply a spirit of curiosity and possibility thinking in relation to the future.

Most excitingly, children's digital play is not something that is static and set. The nature of digital play and what it involves is still under construction. We might think that others are responsible for its construction, such as digital games designers and producers, but this is not the case. The digital play industry responds to the needs and opportunities that practitioners and parents vocalise. By creating a stronger vision around children's digital play, we can make a radical contribution to the future of digital play. I often hear my students saying something like 'children are so lazy now in terms of their imagination; digital technologies just imagine everything for them so that they don't have to'. However, a statement like this suggests that digital play is just what it is and cannot be designed in such a way as to encourage a more imaginative approach among children. Are we so sure that there aren't particular digital play experiences that are deeply imaginative? And even if there are not any currently, would it be so impossible to design a digital play experience that is deeply imaginative? In this respect, we need to be more open, more optimistic and more curious about the future of digital play. As we come to articulate what it is that we want children to experience through their play – including through their digital play – we can have a vital influence on the development of digital play experiences designed for children. So this book is also an experience of brainstorming the future of digital play, so that we can work towards a future of digital play that is truly inspiring.

GOOD REASONS FOR READING THIS BOOK

Readers of this book will be bringing different levels and types of experience. You might be a student of early childhood, you might be a practitioner in an early years setting, or you might see yourself first and foremost as a carer wanting to take a more critical perspective on your children's digital engagement. Regardless of your particular role in relation to young children, you will have picked up this book because you want to make sense of the rise in children's digital play and what it means in relation to play, learning and wellbeing. I hope that you will already have developed some criticality in relation to the common voices you hear in the popular media, and that you are interested in engaging with research, theory, reflections and observations in order to think about digital play more deeply. This book will help you to ask open questions about digital play and engage critically with different forms of evidence and insights that have been generated about children's experiences of digital play. You will probably find by the end of reading the book that you are actually asking more questions about digital play than you did previously. This is excellent – open questions about digital play in a spirit of genuine inquiry are exactly what is needed, and are a great indicator that you are developing academically and even have the potential to carry out research in this field.

HOW TO GET THE MOST OUT OF YOUR READING

This book is not just about 'reading', or at least not as you might think about 'reading' at the moment. It is about actively engaging in a complex dialogue between different forms of knowledge: observations, reflections, cutting-edge research studies, distinct theoretical perspectives and your own primary research findings. Some of the parts of the dialogue will come from the book, but many will come from you. In Table 1.1, you can see how the contributions are divided up between me and you:

Table 1.1 The book as a dialogue

Part of the dialogue	Me	You
Observations of everyday digital play	X	X
Reflections on observations, research, theory and experience		X
Theoretical perspectives on the issues	X	
Summaries of cutting-edge research ('Research Spotlights')	X	
Carrying out primary research		X
Suggestions for further reading and research	X	

You will see from Table 1.1, that there is a back and forth dialogue between the book and you. The more you bring to your part of the dialogue, the more you will get from the book. For example, in a typical chapter you will find that there are observations of everyday experiences among children that help you to see issues applied in a naturalistic context, but as well as the observations that are shared by me, there will also be multiple invitations to you to conduct your own observations. You will find 'Reflection Activities' at various points throughout each chapter; these questions are designed to encourage you to actively respond to what you have read and to apply the ideas to the particular context that you find yourself in. 'Research Spotlight' sections in each chapter summarise cutting-edge research around digital play in relation to the topic of the chapter, but you will also find 'Research Activities' at the end of each chapter with ideas for primary research that you could do yourself around the issue.

Beyond the questions and the activities that are explicitly asked of you, practise bringing your criticality to every single part of what you read. A simple way to do this is to ask yourself the following questions as you read:

- Do I agree?
- Do I find this argument convincing?
- Do I find the evidence for this argument convincing?
- How does this argument relate to my experiences of the world? Does it fit well?
- Do I have a different impression of the issues?
- How has my way of seeing the issue developed as a result of finding out about this argument, perspective or these research findings?

This book is not gospel and all of it should absolutely be questioned by you. This is the only way for you to develop your own critical insights about each topic and about the overall issue of digital play in early childhood. It is much more important that you develop and practise your questioning approach by using this book, than it is that you come away with some new facts or pieces of technical vocabulary.

What does this mean on a practical level? It would be helpful to have a notebook to hand so that you can make notes as you go and respond in writing to the Reflection Activities. If your copy of this book is physical, read it with a pen in your hand and note the parts that resonate with you or that you disagree with. If your copy of this book is electronic, use whatever annotation strategies are available to you to add your own comments in the margin. If this is difficult (e.g. if you are reading while on the move), at least be prepared to pause at the Reflection Activities and consider your response to them.

Many of the Reflection Activities and all of the Research Activities ask you to conduct primary research with children. So think now about the early childhood settings that you have access to, both the formal settings (such as nurseries, playgroups and schools) and the informal settings (the homes of family and friends, and maybe your own home too). How much access do you have when it comes to conducting research in these settings? Flick now through the book to some of the ends of chapters where the Research Activities are outlined; looking at these activities, do you think you will have opportunities to conduct at least some of the Research Activities (even if in a simplified format)? Doing your own primary research around digital play is not crucial, but it can be an excellent way of developing your own critical perspectives on the issue and also developing a more critical eye when it comes to considering the research conducted by others. You may even be a student with your own research project to conduct now or in the coming year(s), in which case the Research Activities might offer you some inspiration.

When we engage in research with children, it is essential that before doing the research we consider a range of ethical issues, and if possible, participate in an ethical approval process in the institution where we are based. Ethical issues range from anonymity and confidentiality, to obtaining parental consent on behalf of young children involved in the research, as well as obtaining informed consent/assent if possible from children themselves. There is not the space here to explore each of these issues in detail, but you will find that ethical considerations are given full discussion in the main textbooks on conducting research as a student of early childhood. If you are a university student, your institution will probably have an ethical approval process that you can participate in. This is essentially someone else checking over your research procedures and instruments and making suggestions about how to ensure that you take all ethical considerations into account as part of your research. If you are not at a university though, there is still scope for developing an ethical approval process in a more informal way. For example, if you are a practitioner in a nursery or school, think about who you can show your research plans to before you conduct the research. Is there someone who has the authority to intervene if they think some of the research is not appropriate or should be modified?

Is there someone who can act as a 'critical friend' as you plan your research, ensuring that you respect the rights of the children, teachers and parents involved in your research? These checks and balances are an essential part of being a researcher, regardless of how much experience you have, so make sure that you write up all your research plans and instruments (e.g. questionnaires, interview or focus group questions, observation prompts) well in advance of your plans to actually collect data. That way, you will be able to share your plans and instruments with others and get their thoughts and ideas before you start the research process. In this way, research is always a social and collaborative process rather than an individual one.

Having said all this, please do not let the ethical issues scare you away from engaging in your own research. I can think of no more transformative experience in the academic and practitioner journey than conducting your own primary research. Not only do you find out new things through research and make your own contributions to knowledge, but you also gain a whole new perspective on what knowledge is and where it comes from. Doing your own research will enable you to develop new levels of criticality, which will resonate through everything you write, read and do in the future.

OVERVIEW OF CHAPTERS

The book is divided into eight main chapters, each of which is introduced briefly below. If there are particular issues that you want to find out more about, you will be able to identify the relevant chapter through the outlines below.

Chapter 2 explores social interaction in relation to digital play. It aims to situate digital technologies in a sociocultural context and then explore aspects of social interaction and how these manifest differently in children's digital play. For example, it focuses on children's collaborative creativity as a facet of play, and examines whether we can see the same levels and types of collaborative creativity when we carry out close observations of children's digital play. The chapter also explores the debate about the constant connectedness offered by online platforms, and whether this enables children to engage in more frequent social interactions or inhibits deeper forms of connection.

In the third chapter, the focus is on physical engagement and sensory experience in the context of digital play. It offers a critical discussion of the view that digital technologies are to blame for children's inactive lifestyles and impoverished sensory experience. It explores the possibilities of new forms of digital play that can help to get children more active and involved in rich sensory experiences, even 'messy play' experiences, while they engage in digital play.

Chapter 4 considers the relationship between outdoor play and digital play and assesses evidence underpinning the idea that digital play is to blame for the decline of outdoor play among children. It also introduces a more theoretical debate between those who see digital technologies as getting in the way of children's deepest play instincts, and those who argue that technologies have always been a part of humans' existence (and therefore children's play) and that digital technologies are a continuation of this.

Chapter 5 examines how imagination manifests in digital play environments and whether it is fair to think of children's imaginations as impoverished in digital play environments. You might remember I mentioned that many of my students often level this claim at digital play. The chapter introduces the concepts of possibility thinking, 'remix', 'mash-up' and transgressive play to help us think about imagination and creativity in children's digital play. You will see that these concepts help us to spot old and new forms of imagination and creativity when we conduct close observations of children engaged in digital play.

In the sixth chapter, the focus is on how digital play relates to children's media literacy. The chapter explores two sides of children's digital play: how it simultaneously seems to facilitate agency and autonomy among children, and how it also means that children are increasingly targeted as consumers by multinational corporations. The chapter explores the essential role that adults have in helping children to develop their media literacy, so that they enhance their autonomy while also engaging in digital play in safe ways and with a critical gaze on what they come across.

Chapter 7 discusses what we know about how attention as an aspect of cognition is changed as a result of engaging frequently in digital play environments. It explores the psychological research that suggests that there are particular 'cognitive shifts' arising from the rise of digital engagement, and goes on to examine the proposed link between digital play and diagnoses of attention deficit and hyperactivity disorder (ADHD). It discusses whether fast-paced environments are an inevitable aspect of digital play, and what slower forms of digital play for children might look like – and indeed, whether any such sloweddown forms of digital play currently exist.

Chapter 8 asks what the consequences of digital play are for children's emerging sense of self. It explores how the self can come about through children's digital practices, and the helpful distinction between self-presentation and self-representation when thinking about our engagement with different types of digital environment.

The aim of Chapter 9 is to put digital play into its wider context. In doing this, the chapter examines the role of the adult in relation to children's digital play, and the wider discourses that surround children's digital play and how these in turn influence our mediation on a day-to-day basis. Finally the chapter discusses the importance of challenging how we think about what digital play actually is, and the need to question whether the term should even be used.

The conclusion chapter at the end of the book highlights key themes that run across all the previous chapters. These themes help us to think about the next steps we need to take in research, practice and even in our personal lives. In particular it highlights 1) the need to appreciate the complexity of digital play and the many layers it involves, 2) the value of engaging in possibility thinking around what digital play involves and might involve in the future, 3) how we can positively influence children's engagement in digital play, helping them to develop curiosity and criticality, and finally 4) the urgent need for our own approach to digital play to embody the 3Cs: criticality, creativity and curiosity.

2
DIGITAL TECHNOLOGIES AND SOCIAL INTERACTION

INTRODUCTION

In this chapter we explore the relationship between digital technologies and social interaction in the context of children's play. This chapter will:

- situate digital technologies in a sociocultural context, and invite you to explore specific technologies through the concept of affordances;
- explore two particular aspects of social interaction that emerge as important in the context of children's play: collaborative creativity and affective alignment;
- examine how different digital technologies appear to feed into instances of collaborative creativity and affective alignment between individuals as they engage in play;
- consider the argument that the constant connectedness of online platforms gives rise to particular forms of instant social interaction that inhibit deeper forms of connection;
- discuss the counter-argument that online platforms actually enable children to engage in new meaningful social interactions through technologies that connect us over great distances.

Throughout the chapter, you are encouraged to conduct your own observations and write your own reflections on the relationship between digital technologies and social interaction. The chapter explores theoretical concepts through observations of children playing with digital technologies, and it also introduces specific pieces of primary research through 'Research Spotlights' in order to show how the theoretical perspectives and concepts we have considered can be applied in empirical research.

CASE STUDY 2.1

PLAYING ON THE INTERACTIVE WHITEBOARD DURING 'CHOOSING TIME'

The following fieldnotes come from a small-scale observation study in which I observed 4–5-year-old children in a classroom as they engaged with the Interactive Whiteboard (IWB) during free-flow activity time (known in the class as 'choosing time'). I captured observations through video recordings on the videocamera and iPad, and made written fieldnotes based on my impressions gathered during each day over the course of 1 week. The following excerpt comes from the fieldnotes made on the first day of data collection. They suggest lots of ways in which the children's use of the IWB is guided through the set-up of the resources and the support they receive from adults in doing activities on the IWB. These fieldnotes help us to think about how the sociocultural context gives children messages about how to use digital technologies as part of their social interactions in play.

. . .

When it comes to 'choosing time', there are many activities for the children to choose from – laid out in special ways – for example, treasure maps for inspiration at the writing table, along with paper that has the edges burnt so that it looks old. On the planning outline for the week, it says what resources are part of 'continuous provision'. No digital technologies are mentioned on this, even though the teacher tells me that playing on the IWB is always an option for the children during choosing time, unless the board is not working.

In the morning, the IWB is on and connected to the internet. A website called 'ICT Games' is loaded on the screen. Within this, a basic literacy game has been selected. It is a 'look and spell' game where short sight words are presented on the inside of a toilet lid, then hidden in the toilet, and the children have to remember which letters were in the word and pick these from some options, drag them down, and then flush to check whether they're correct.

Next to the IWB is a small table that has lots of the teachers' papers and resources on it. Also placed on this table is a sand-timer. Most of the children do not use the sand-timer,

(Continued)

though some turn the sand-timer at the start of their turn, or point to the sand-timer to suggest that it's time for someone else to have a go.

How do the children play the game on the IWB? They line up to take turns. Those queuing sometimes make suggestions about what should be done next, but these are generally ignored. There is a noticeable lack of collaboration – they are not solving each problem together, but just waiting for their turn. When they line up, they are often crowding the person that is actually using the board.

One of the immediately obvious issues with using the IWB is the height of the board – the children are having to stretch and sometimes ask me to help them to get letters that are towards the corners of the board. This breaks the flow of the activity. They have a box to stand on, but it is placed under the centre of the board, so that it doesn't help if they're reaching towards the left or the right.

At lunchtime I ask the teacher whether it would be ok for me to download the free art-making software Tux Paint as an example of open-ended application to see how the children will interact with a digital resource that encourages more engagement through free-flow play.

After lunch it's choosing time again. I model using Tux Paint on the IWB and this interests a few children. They have a go with the shapes and paintbrush and the eraser. More children arrive and there is more of a demand to have a go – the lining up happens again, making it claustrophobic for the primary user. There is little joint decision-making. Instead when one of the children has an idea, they come to the computer itself and try to use the mousepad to change what's happening. I have to keep reminding them that it won't work if lots of people are trying to use the board at the same time. Having said this, I'm also keen for them to be a bit more collaborative in their approach. I try to encourage them not to line up and instead just to keep in mind whose turn it is, but they don't like this – they seem to think it will mean that they will lose their turn. There's a little bit of pushing in the queue.

DIGITAL TECHNOLOGIES IN A SOCIOCULTURAL CONTEXT

Sociocultural theory places the focus on how the activities we engage in are mediated by the social, cultural and material contexts in which they unfold. So the social nature of children's play will depend not only on the particular physical properties of the tools they are playing with, whether these are digital or non-digital, and what is physically possible; but also the social and cultural messages that surround the tools and suggest what would be an appropriate form of engagement. Together, these social associations and physical properties are called 'affordances'. The concept 'affordances' was first used by the ecological psychologist J.J. Gibson, to describe how our perception of the environment is always action-based; that is, as a result of affordances, we are always perceiving the best functions and uses of the objects around us rather than developing an objective notion of what surrounds us (Gibson, 1961). In this perspective, a path is not just a path; the path is perceived as the affordance of walking on that path. Similarly, a chair is not just a chair; the chair is perceived as the affordance of sitting. In social semiotic theory, a sociocultural approach that focuses particularly on acts of communication, these two types of message about how technologies should be used – the social associations and the physical features – are brought together in the concept of 'affordances' (Bezemer & Kress, 2015). For example, lined paper and biro pens are perceived as affording the action of writing. This is a result of physical properties (e.g. the lines that guide our writing) and cultural investment (e.g. the many times we have seen lined paper used for writing).

If we believe that children engaging in digital play are more likely to be playing alone than cooperatively, we need to unpick why this might be the case by looking at the affordances of digital technologies – in terms of both the physical properties of the technologies and the cultural messages that surround them. In the fieldnotes above, solitary engagement as opposed to collaboration appears to be facilitated by the way in which the IWB accepts only a single input at any one time (a physical property). If multiple users try to physically interact with the IWB at the same time, the device will stop responding and the interaction will break down. As the only adult around at this particular moment and known to the children through my participation in the class over the course of a week, I warned the children that they should not interact with the laptop computer when someone else was using the IWB. I did this because I was worried about technical difficulties, but the result was a cultural message about the importance of turn-taking (as opposed to collaboration) when incorporating the IWB in play.

In the fieldnotes above, some important affordances of the IWB include:

- the need for single-user input for the board to be responsive;
- the height of the IWB and the fact that only one child could stand on the stool at a time to reach the upper half of the board;
- the positioning of the IWB under sunlight, which makes it difficult to see the visual activity unfolding on the board;
- my directions about using the board carefully;
- the placement of a sand-timer next to the IWB, which suggests the need for turn-taking and self-awareness among children about the duration of their engagement with the IWB and the possibility that others want to have a turn;
- the general commitment in early childhood education contexts to promoting turn-taking, fairness and sharing among young children.

Together, these properties and associations afford mostly solitary, or at least uncollaborative, playful engagement among children.

It is important to recognise, though, that the relationship is two-way: the sociocultural context of the early years classroom shapes how digital technologies are taken up as part of social interactions in children's play, but simultaneously the presence of and engagement with the digital technologies in the environment of the classroom is part of the ever-changing sociocultural context of the classroom. This is articulated by Burnett (2014) in her concept of 'classroom-ness', which she uses to explain how classrooms constrain how digital technologies are taken up (e.g. through the emphasis on turn-taking as opposed to collaboration), but also how the resources available in the space shape the associations of the space over time. The IWB in the classroom described above has the potential to change how turn-taking is perceived and enacted. Perhaps as children take the risk of collaborating around the IWB, which has at least some physical properties that enable and encourage collaboration (e.g. the large size of the working surface), this will impact on practices more widely in the classroom, and lead to new forms of cooperation and collaboration in play throughout the space – not just at the IWB.

It is important to note also that the IWB in the particular classroom that features in the fieldnotes is not listed in the planning documents created by practitioners as 'continuous provision'. This might suggest that it is not seen as offering 'real' play or learning experiences that feature planning. The scepticism of practitioners in early childhood education around the potential of digital technologies to be involved in 'real play' has been documented in the research of Edwards (2013, 2016). Edwards argues that practitioners are so used to seeing children's play mediated through non-digital tools, that this has led to practitioners struggling to envisage and associate free-flow play unfolding through digital technologies. As a result, they may dismiss digital play and fail to plan for enhanced social interactions through digital play. To counter this, Edwards (2016) offers a web-mapping tool to practitioners that enables them to document the connections that run across children's online and offline play, so that digital play is seen in the context of children's play practices more generally, rather than perceived as distinct altogether and somehow not quite 'real'. When taking this approach, it may be easier to imagine how practitioners might be more aware of how digital technologies such as the IWB are integrated in children's free-flow play activity, and how particular forms of social interaction, such as collaboration, could perhaps be encouraged in situations of digital play.

RESEARCH SPOTLIGHT

Plowman, L., Stephen, C., & McPake, J. (2010). Supporting young children's learning with technology at home and in preschool. *Research Papers in Education*, 25(1), 93–113.

AIMS

This study investigated how children's use of technologies is supported in the home and the preschool. The study is framed through sociocultural theory, and applies the sociocultural concept of 'guided interaction' to understand the similarities and differences between how children's technology use is facilitated through interactions with adults in the home and the preschool environment. The research aimed to observe how guided interaction unfolds in either setting. The researchers considered both proximal guided interaction (face to face) and distal guided interaction (how adults resource the environment and set up activities). Plowman et al. focused on non-verbal modes of behaviour, since their previous research had noted a lack of talk in preschools between adults and children when it came to interacting around technologies.

METHODS

The research draws on two studies, both looking at the experiences of 3–4 year olds when using technologies. The first study involved eight preschools; in each of these preschool environments, the researchers made video observations of children's engagement with technologies and interviewed practitioners about their support for children's use of technology. The second study involved a survey of 346 parents and 24 case study families who were visited five times over 15 months and were observed and interviewed with regard to their use of technologies. Based on the data, the researchers compared their findings in respect of how guided interaction occurred in the home and preschool environments.

FINDINGS

The researchers found that the home environment was characterised by a more diverse range of technologies available to children, a higher level of general support for children's use of technologies, and that this included children engaged in more observation of others (siblings, parents/carers) involved in using technologies to fulfil personal objectives. Children in the home observed their older siblings using technology as an embedded part of their social lives, for example taking photographs through their mobile phones, texting their friends and accessing music to share with others. They observed their parents using technology as a part of their everyday life as well, from ordering shopping to booking holidays. The preschool environment in comparison was characterised by a lack of integration of technology into authentic activities, that is, activities that have a cultural and personal purpose, rather than a purely educational purpose. There was less modelling of technology use in the preschool environment, while in the home, modelling tended to unfold in a context of shared enjoyment and parents were not always aware that they were involved in modelling the use of technologies to their children. The researchers also found a lack of communication between preschool contexts and the home environment about children's use of technology. There was some disregard among practitioners for the rich experiences that children were having in the home around technology.

REFLECTION ACTIVITIES

- Think about the digital technologies that you own. What sociocultural messages surround each of these devices? What constitutes appropriate use for each of those devices? Which ones are better suited to solitary activities? Which do you associate more with effective collaboration? How have you come to these conclusions – through experience, through observation of others or through advertising?

- Keep a diary of your digital technology (DT) use for 24 hours. Chart how the digital technologies that you use are embedded in the sociocultural context. To do this, describe what you are doing on the DT each time you engage with it, but then also what social context is surrounding this use, for example your purpose, where you are, when you are using the DT and who you are with.

- Based on your diary, write a reflection on the way that DTs are part of your social interactions in an everyday way. What kinds of social connection do they encourage? What kinds of social interaction do they inhibit? Would this be the same for young children?

CASE STUDY 2.2

MAKING COMPUTER ART TOGETHER: A MILLION CUCKOOS

M (3 years old) and her father (D) are making art together on a laptop computer through the software Tux Paint. In the following segment of activity, they are playing with the 'stamp' tool available in Tux Paint. This tool allows you to select an image (either a cartoon image or a photographic image) and apply this image to the screen as many times as you like.

M leans forward to look at the stamps available and points to a photographic image of a cuckoo. She says 'yellow one' while pointing.

D has the mouse now. He selects the cuckoo image and moves the mouse so that the image is hovering about the canvas in Tux Paint. He presses down and the computer makes the 'cuckoo' sound as the image is deposited onto the canvas.

D: Cuckoo?

M: Yeah

D: That's a cuckoo

M: Oh, a cuckoo

   [D stamps the image again onto the screen two more times]

> D: Three cuckoos
>
>> [D continues to place cuckoo stamps onto the screen, M leans forward watching]
>
> D: Shall I do a million cuckoos? [laughs]
>
> M: You can [seriously]
>
>> [D and M watch the screen avidly in silence. D continues to put stamps on the screen]
>>
>> [D takes his hand away from the mouse]
>
> D: How about that? That's a million
>
>> [D looks down at M who leans up towards him. They make eye contact with each other]
>
> M: No there's one more to make a million
>
>> [D laughs and passes the mouse across to M]
>
> D: You do the one more wherever you like

HOW IS COLLABORATIVE CREATIVITY IN PLAY MEDIATED BY DIGITAL TECHNOLOGIES?

Since 2000, there has been an increasing focus on the social nature of creativity, which contrasts with traditional psychological models that posit creativity to be an individual capacity. Glăveanu (2010, 2017) has written extensively about what he refers to as the 'We-paradigm' of creativity. This is a perspective on creativity that explores and homes in on the social and material environment in which creativity unfolds. The 'We-paradigm' is supported by a large body of research looking at how creative processes are fostered in groups (e.g. Fiedler, 1962; Abric, 1971; Siau, 1995; Paulus & Nijstad, 2003; Sawyer, 2004, 2011). When looking at creativity in children's everyday practices, researchers such as Hämäläinen and Vähäsantanen (2011) and Burnard and Younker (2008) have applied 'We-paradigm' thinking, and explored creativity as a network of activity that occurs as a dialogue between two or more children and the material and cultural elements of the context around them.

Put simply, collaborative creativity can be thought about as the sharing of an idea between two or more individuals. This is a fundamental part of cooperative play between children, when, for example, they take an idea for a role play and develop it through a flowing interaction together. While the definition of collaborative creativity as a 'shared idea' is often associated with communication through speech, it is important to think about the other modes of communication that are drawn into collaborative creativity. We need to fully explore facial expressions, body positions, touch, gesture and non-linguistic utterances (such as laughter) as part of how collaborative creativity unfolds between children in situations of play (Vass, 2007; Grossen, 2008; Rojas-Drummond, Albarrán & Littleton, 2008). In the observation of the child and her father above, the collaborative creativity is not just unfolding through their speech. We see important moments of shared gaze that contribute significantly to the collaborative creativity. There is also the manipulation of the tools themselves – how the mouse is passed between the child and her father, which sets up a physical sense of ideas moving back and forth between the two individuals, which in turn contributes to the collaborative creativity. The laughter that punctuates the observation is also important – it shows the shared positive affect between the child and her father, which acts as a foundation for the collaborative creativity that unfolds.

How collaborative creativity – in all its multimodal richness – unfolds will depend on the resources that are used as part of the interaction. In the observation, the laptop computer, with input through a mouse, and the software Tux Paint are part of the collaborative creativity and impact on how the creativity unfolds as a result of the physical properties and social associations of the technologies (the 'affordances', as explained in the section above on the sociocultural context; see p. 14). We can have an idea about what affordances of digital technologies might be important in shaping collaborative creativity in children's play before we even observe the technologies in use. At the same time, we need to maintain our capacity to be surprised by what we observe about how affordances are 'actualised' through use (Björkvall & Engblom, 2010). Some design features of particular digital technologies might seem not to support collaborative creativity, but how these features play out in actual interactions might not be what we would expect. For example, Wohlwend (2017a) conducted observations of children engaged in playing through the app Puppet Pals on the iPad. She had expected that the small size of the iPad screen might be problematic for collaborative creativity, and she was surprised by the way that the children engaged together despite this. She was struck by the jumble of hands and touch over the screen, the apparent 'messiness' of the social interaction, but as she looked closely at the interaction as it unfolded moment by moment, she became aware of the extent to which the collaborative creativity in the play was there, and was from the children's point of view a successful aspect of the interaction. This suggests that digital technologies perhaps do not need to facilitate 'tidy' turn-taking in order to support collaborative creativity.

In the observation above, how is collaborative creativity mediated by the digital technology of the laptop computer? The child and her father in this part of the activity take turns in quite a controlled way using the mouse, which is the main input device for the computer (the other being the touchpad on the computer itself, which they do not use). To begin with, the involvement of the child comes through the unfolding multimodal dialogue (conducted through speech, facial expressions, gaze, laughter) rather than physical engagement with the computer. At the end of the observation, the father involves the child actively with the physical resources by passing her the mouse. This is different from the IWB, which is activated through touch on a large inviting vertical surface. The mouse is a physically more contained input device, leading to more confined turn-taking behaviours, but perhaps this frees up the rest of the multimodal communication so that the collaborative creativity through speech, laughter, gesture, facial expression, gaze and body position can be more open and sustained. The important thing to bear in mind is how particular the affordances of distinct digital technologies will be. For each digital technology there will be particular affordances to consider theoretically, and these will then be actualised in different ways at different times and in different spaces. This means that there can be no blanket statements about how digital technologies impact on collaborative creativity, or whether digital play supports or inhibits collaborative creativity.

RESEARCH SPOTLIGHT

Wohlwend, K.E. (2015). One screen, many fingers: Young children's collaborative literacy play with digital puppetry apps and touchscreen technologies. *Theory Into Practice, 54*(2), 154–162.

AIMS

This study explored how digital literacy practices unfold as part of children's collaboration via a digital puppetry app on a touchscreen device. Stemming from a new literacies perspective, the paper reflects on how children's interaction as part of this experience helps us to integrate digital technologies into our understanding of children's literacy. It argues that our concept of literacy needs to change in order to incorporate the developments in how children make meaning through collaborative creative tasks via digital technologies.

METHODS

The paper describes an observation of three young children (ages unspecified) as they engage together with the app Puppet Pals on an iPad. A video recording was made of the observation, and close attention was paid to short segments of the interaction in order to observe the multiple layers of the collaboration, which involved a wide range of modes – both embodied modes (touch, manipulation, gesture, gaze, body orientation and so on) and the disembodied modes that could be used as part of the app (voiceovers, sound effects, movement around the screen, selection of characters and so on).

(Continued)

FINDINGS

Wohlwend suggests that while observations such as this can appear chaotic and crowded, when we look carefully at what is going on, we can see in-depth literacy learning emerging as part of successful social interactions. Children are engaged in complex processes of collaboration with each other, organising their own bodily resources in order to go about the task, and demonstrating an in-depth and growing understanding of how creative texts are produced and enhanced. Wohlwend argues that bodily resources that we might take for granted in digital touchscreen environments – such as swiping, dragging and using two fingers to zoom into the screen – are actually key parts of digital literacy. In addition, through this kind of experience, children are understanding how 'story meanings [are] deepened by the layered meanings represented simultaneously through speech, image, action, music and sound effects' (p. 158). Based on these observations, Wohlwend suggests that adults can better support children's collaborative creativity in digital contexts by selecting open-ended apps that support playful collaborations rather than settling for apps that are based on an 'old' definition of literacy and focus entirely on print decoding. Building on this, adults can enhance learning environments by creating 'playshops' (Wohlwend, 2013) in the classroom, which bring together a wide variety of resources, digital and non-digital, that children can use in a playful, collaborative exploration of their ideas. Playshops are designed to 'bridge literacy practices, play, and children's multimedia knowledge' (p. 160). Adopting this approach to integrating technologies into learning environments places an emphasis on collaborative creativity, and embraces the role that digital technologies play in what literacy is and will be in the lives of children growing up today.

REFLECTION ACTIVITIES

- Video yourself engaged in a collaborative creative task on a phone or on a tablet with a friend. Use a creative open-ended app, such as Puppet Pals (featured in the Research Spotlight above).

- Before re-viewing the video, reflect afterwards on the experience of the collaborative task. Did the app and/or device support collaborative creativity? Compare your reflections with those of your partner.

- Now watch the video back. How does the video recording support what you and/or your partner felt about the experience? Can you identify specific moments when collaborative creativity was supported or stifled by features of the digital technology? If so, what were the nature of these features – were they physical properties of the device, or were they more the result of your expectations and assumptions about what it was appropriate to do?

DIGITAL TECHNOLOGIES AND SOCIAL INTERACTION   23

CASE STUDY 2.3

DRAWING TOGETHER ON THE IPAD

Figure 2.1   Drawing together on the iPad – first frame

L (on the right) watches while T draws intently on the iPad. He shows concentration through his posture, leaning in towards the drawing, and his intent gaze. L demonstrates interest by maintaining gaze on the drawing. Her clasped hands suggest that she is inhibiting her own movement and giving T the space to do his part of the drawing without interference.

Figure 2.2   Drawing together on the iPad – second frame

(Continued)

Once T decides that he has finished his part of the drawing, he pushes the iPad back over to L so that she can continue the drawing. She is wondering what to add to the drawing, and her gesture echoes this questioning. L and T both maintain gaze on the iPad, suggesting that they are both still interested in the task and collectively invested in the outcome.

Figure 2.3 Drawing together on the iPad – third frame

At the start of the second drawing, T is wondering what to draw. Still thinking about what to draw, L and T mirror the body positions of one another. They both adopt a typical 'thinking' pose, putting a hand somewhere on their head or face, and turning their gaze towards the distance. Although they are not looking at one another and their gaze is distributed, the mirrored posture and actions suggest that they are attuned to one another in the activity.

Figure 2.4 Drawing together on the iPad – fourth frame

> The colour of the drawing on the screen changes. This leads to both participants simultaneously moving backwards away from the screen. Their facial expressions demonstrate their shared surprise at how the drawing has changed. Their physical mirroring suggests closeness and that they are both invested in how the drawing is changing.

HOW IS AFFECTIVE ALIGNMENT MEDIATED BY DIGITAL TECHNOLOGIES?

Affective alignment is another important dimension of social interaction in free-flow play. It refers to when we feel emotionally attuned to another person, that is, we feel like we are on the 'same page' as one another. According to the research on communication of Charles and Marjorie Goodwin, affective alignment is a visible phenomenon that we can see playing out through the various modes involved in face-to-face interaction, including gaze, facial expression, body position and so on (Goodwin, 2006, 2007). We can tell whether individuals are affectively aligned with one another through how they organise their bodies and how they move in relation to each other. Moments of heightened affective alignment can be called 'moments of meeting', a term originally used by the infant psychologist Stern (2000, 2004) to refer to moments shared between a young child and their carer where they show an intense emotional closeness. Examples of moments of meeting in everyday contexts would be when two individuals break into shared laughter at the same time, or when one individual is supported by another to do something that they would otherwise be too fearful to do (e.g. sliding down a slide). Affective alignment, and moments of meeting, are fundamental aspects of collaborative free-flow play between children. Children who are playing together might not always be affectively aligned, but they will move through fluctuations in the level of affective alignment, with peaks that resemble moments of meeting.

What are the moments of meeting in the observation above? We can see various ways in which the multimodal interaction plays out to suggest that there is affective alignment. The digital technology – in this case, the iPad and the particular drawing app selected for engagement – features in how this affective alignment plays out. For example, the children are affectively aligned when their bodies simultaneously jump backwards indicating shared surprise about what has appeared on the screen. This moment of meeting, demonstrated through the physical mimicry of the children's bodies, comes about through the elements of visual surprise that are built into this particular app on the iPad. In this drawing app, the colour and texture of the line changes spontaneously, without the user manually selecting the change. If they had been drawing on paper instead, using pencils, this element of surprise would not have occurred, and there would not have been the affective alignment that manifested as shared surprise. Of course, this is not to say that all digital technologies, or even all apps on the iPad, will encourage moments like this – but just that, if the element of surprise is built into the free-flow digital resources that children use, moments like this are more likely to arise.

Sakr and Kucirkova (2017) explored, through observational research, how moments of meeting and affective alignment are shaped by different semiotic resources, digital and non-digital, identifying a series of specific ways in which distinct technologies can contribute to affective alignment or disalignment. Based on the research, they argued that there is no neat distinction to be made between digital and non-digital resources. Instead, to understand how digital technologies can shape affective alignment, we need to look at particular technologies in particular contexts of use. This means picking apart the network of affordances that surround particular resources, and also maintaining the potential to be surprised by how affordances are 'actualised' through everyday practices (Björkvall & Engblom, 2010). We might think that a particular app on the iPad will be supportive of affective alignment and moments of meeting, but when we observe it in use, we are surprised to see that the children engaged with the device are not supported in developing a closer social connection.

REFLECTION ACTIVITIES

- Look back at the video of yourself engaging in a collaborative creative task with a friend. This time, makes notes on affective alignment. Are there particularly intense moments of affective alignment (moments of meeting), or are there moments when the affective alignment is notably absent and your engagement appears to visibly move away from that of your friend?

- Now analyse these particular segments of the video in more detail. How is the technology (both the device and the app/software you are using) involved in the patterns of affective alignment? Are the resources supporting affective alignment? If so, how? Are the resources getting in the way of affective alignment? If so, how?

- Are there different digital resources that you feel might have better supported affective alignment in this collaborative creative task? Perhaps, after re-viewing the video, you wonder whether a device with a larger screen, or an app that prompted more shared positive affect (e.g. demonstrated through more giggling), might have been better. If you have ideas about this, why not put them to the test by videoing yourself completing a different collaborative creative task with these resources, and seeing whether your ideas play out in reality?

CASE STUDY 2.4

CONVERSATIONS ABOUT ALEXA WITH A 7 YEAR OLD

R = Researcher
M = Child
A = Alexa

R: What is Alexa? Say you had a friend who had never heard of Alexa before and she came to your house and saw Alexa. How would explain Alexa to her?

M: It's a small robot. You can get it small or big-sized. Different colours maybe, which are grey or white. Alexa is a girl . . .

A: Sorry I didn't catch that.

M: Alexa [whispers so that Alexa doesn't pick up on this as a command] is a woman, who, is a woman, her voice is a woman, a normal woman, maybe, a polite woman. She . . . she . . . plays music, plays bands, answers questions, gives you facts and can make you laugh. She's nice company and a good friend.

R: So is she like a computer?

M: Yes, it's like a mini-computer put into a shape . . . a sphere . . . a cylinder.

R: Where everything is talking?

M: Yeh. And put into the cylinder.

R: And would you recommend her to your friends?

M: Yeh, I think it's better than Sira, Siri? And the other one. Because do they say jokes and?

R: I'm not sure.

M: Well I think it might just be a better company and I support Amazon and I think it's a good . . . I just think it's really nice to have a friend.

R: So do you think of Alexa as a friend?

M: Sometimes yeh.

R: Because she keeps you company . . .?

M: Yeh, anyone who keeps me company can be my friend.

CONNECTEDNESS VERSUS CONNECTION

An important aspect of children's play is connecting with others in the 'here and now'. As Bruce (1991) describes, through play children 'wallow' in ideas, thoughts and feelings. The verb 'wallow' gives a strong sense of the importance of sinking into the moment and giving yourself over to it fully. So what happens to this aspect of play when connection is made possible on multiple levels simultaneously as a result of the constant connectedness of digital technologies (through the internet)? In the transcript of the conversation about Alexa above, what is the nature of the connection between the child and Alexa? The child describes playing with Alexa and thinking of Alexa as her friend, since Alexa keeps her company. In what ways is this similar to or dissimilar from the types of connection we consider play to be promoting more traditionally? Is Alexa really a friend? Is the device enabling or preventing 'wallowing', or is it just part of the play context in which the wallowing unfolds?

These questions relate to popular concerns that digital technologies are hindering children to connect fully with those around them (Wooldridge & Shapka, 2012; Steiner-Adair & Barker, 2013; Turkle, 2017). In popular media, there is a flurry of negative attention surrounding children's interactions with digital technologies, suggesting that children are engaged increasingly in passive preoccupation with digital technologies through game-playing and video-watching, and that this is unfolding at the expense of an intent engagement with the world around them (Gray, 2011; Palmer, 2015). Turkle (2017) in particular argues that we over-invest in the connections we forge and maintain in digital environments; we are increasingly drawn towards these social interactions because they tend to be less emotionally complex than the immediate connections that we have with others who are part of our everyday lives. Thus, our connectedness through digital environments becomes an escape route from genuine social connection.

On the other hand, we need to be open to the ways in which digital technologies might make possible some social interactions that otherwise could not be maintained. As the Research Spotlight below shows, there is the possibility through online platforms such as Skype and Facetime for intergenerational relationships to be maintained across long distances. Earlier research by Mavers (2007) focused on a 7 year old's email messaging of her uncle and how the child, Kathleen, re-shaped and actualised the resources she was using in order to suit her desire for social connection. Mavers documented how Kathleen shook off the expectations of the adults around her and used the medium of email to communicate with her uncle in a more immediate and less formalised way, not adhering to the conventions of writing that she would be concerned about if writing a letter to post. From this perspective, we might get excited about the potentials of digital technologies to open up connections for children that they might not otherwise have access to. The forms of connection that arise in play as a result of these possibilities might look a little different, but different is not the same as 'less than'.

RESEARCH SPOTLIGHT

Kelly, C. (2015). 'Let's do some jumping together': Intergenerational participation in the use of remote technology to co-construct social relations over distance. *Journal of Early Childhood Research*, *13*(1), 29–46.

AIMS

This research focused on how extended family relationships are developed and maintained through Skype despite long distances. It looks particularly at the inter-subjectivity of a young girl (aged 2 at the start of the study, and 4 by the end) in the UK and her grandparents in Australia. It adopts a sociocultural approach to the interaction and how children's interactions may be guided in non-formal learning contexts through various modes and resources. Juxtaposed with this emphasis on the adult's role in non-formal learning, there is a focus on the agency of children in developing patterns of interaction and maintaining relationships.

METHODS

The paper reports on a small-scale longitudinal study that focused on a single family based in the UK and Australia. Skype encounters involving the children and parents (in the UK) and the grandparents (in Australia) were filmed, transcribed and analysed with a focus on the multimodal (verbal and nonverbal) interaction. In addition to these observations, adult participants were interviewed about their experiences and all participants were encouraged to keep reflective diaries. The principal researcher has both an insider and outsider role in this research study, since she is one of the grandparents. She was therefore not only involved in many of the Skype encounters, but also adopted more of an outsider perspective when it came to interpreting and analysing the data generated through the study.

FINDINGS

The observations in the research demonstrated how by the end of the study, when the child was four, she was showing impressive creativity in how she would use the affordances of Skype communication to engage in play with her grandparents and thereby foster closeness with extended family. She increasingly embedded play in the Skype encounters. These play behaviours ranged from doing jumping together on her bed, playing hide and seek, and engaging in pretend play together. For example, in one episode, the girl initiated a pretend play scenario that involved pretending to go camping, building a tent

(Continued)

together with her mother, taking the computer into the tent so that it was as if the grandparents were with her in the tent, and then all pretending to sleep in the tent. In comparison, her younger brother struggled more with finding successful ways to integrate the Skype communication into the kinds of interaction he wanted to engage in with his grandparents. He was more tactile, trying to kiss the screen or offer his grandparents a drink from his cup through the screen. These interactions would have the unwanted effect of ending the call, and could lead to frustration. The observations also showed high levels of scaffolding by the parents. The parents explained in the interviews that they were working hard to try and support the social flow of the interaction on both sides of the Skype call. This meant in practice that there was a high density of verbal scaffolding behaviours, with the parents helping the children to clarify what they wanted to say and needing to get to 'the point' because of the time constraints of this kind of communication.

REFLECTION ACTIVITIES

- Keep a diary of your social interactions through digital technologies over 24 hours. To do this, set a timer on your phone to go off every hour. When the timer goes off, jot down ways in which you have interacted socially through digital technologies over the last hour. For each of these interactions, chart the kinds of connections that unfolded through this digital interaction (examples would be messaging a friend, 'liking' something on a social media site, 'chatting' online to a customer advisor while buying something online, posting a photograph online, etc.). For these different activities, write down details of who you were connecting to, in what way you were connecting, and how meaningful that connection felt to you. Also give a number between 1 and 10 to chart the levels of intimacy and satisfaction that you associated with each of these interactions.

- Respond to Turkle's claim that we are losing our capacity to engage in the messiness of genuine intimacy as a result of our over-engagement with social media platforms. Do you agree? What evidence do you see of this? What do you see to the contrary? Organise your thoughts into arguments for and arguments against Turkle's claim.

CHAPTER SUMMARY

- Digital technologies are part of an ever-changing 'sociotechnical environment' (Bruce, 1997). This means that it does not make sense to ask what 'effect' digital technologies have on children's social interactions as part of their play. Instead, we can think about digital technologies and the nature of children's social interactions as aspects of society that are in constant flux; they are both inextricably intertwined and constantly changing.

- While digital technologies do not affect social interaction in recognisable ways, particular digital technologies can shape social interactions in particular situations as a result of their affordances. Affordance is a concept from social semiotic theory that relates to the physical properties of technologies (and how these shape interaction) as well as the cultural messages that surround the technologies and suggest how we should be engaging with them.

- The research of Edwards (2013, 2016) suggests that in many early childhood settings, digital play is not seen as 'real play' by practitioners. Because of this, there is less awareness about the cultural messages that surround digital technologies in relation to social interaction, and less active planning about how digital technologies will be integrated into the social dimensions of children's play experiences. For example, research in early years classrooms suggests that digital technologies are often laid out with the assumption that children engage with them one by one, taking turns, rather than using the resources collaboratively.

- Theories of collaborative creativity focus on how creative processes occur through multimodal interactions between individuals, situated in the material and cultural environment. Collaborative creativity in play can be thought about as the sharing of an idea by two or more children, but it is important to remember that this sharing process can unfold through nonverbal modes (e.g. gaze, body position, facial expression, gesture and so on) as well as through speech. How collaborative creativity unfolds in children's play will be shaped by the affordances of the physical resources that are used in the play. If digital technologies are part of the play, their particular affordances (which will depend on what the technology is – both the hardware and the software) will shape the collaborative creative processes.

- While we can make predictions about the affordances of particular digital technologies and how these will shape collaborative creativity, we need to leave space for surprise. For example, we might think that a small screen device (such as an iPad or mobile phone) would inhibit collaborative creativity, since two or more individuals would struggle to see the screen, but then in practice, observations have suggested that the opposite can be true (see Wohlwend, 2015, 2017a). Thus, how digital technologies afford activity and interaction can be different from what we would expect.

- Affective alignment is emotional attunement and closeness made visible through multimodal interaction. Moments of meeting are particularly heightened instances of affective alignment. Just as with collaborative creativity in play, affective alignment in play will be mediated by the resources used. Affordances of digital technologies will shape how the affective alignment unfolds. However, research suggests that there is not a neat distinction between digital and non-digital resources. Both types of technology can enable moments of meeting, depending on the specific affordances they possess.

(Continued)

- Some researchers argue that the constant connectedness of online platforms prevents us from engaging fully with social interaction that is unfolding in the here and now. In terms of children's play, we might be concerned that children's online connectedness gets in the way of 'wallowing' behaviours in play (Bruce, 1991), whereby children use play as a way to sink into their thoughts, feelings and ideas and give themselves time and space to process the difficulties or uncertainties in their everyday lives.
- On the other hand, observational research has documented how platforms such as Skype and Facetime give children the opportunity to play across long distances, opening up social interactions and important relationships that might not otherwise be accessible to them.

RESEARCH ACTIVITIES

- Map the use of digital technologies in a classroom or home in which young children are learning. Map not just what technologies are used, but how they are part of the wider sociocultural context. Are children using the digital technologies alone, together, with each other or with an adult? What cultural messages and/or physical properties of the technologies can you see that are feeding into how they feature in social interactions?
- Interview parents/practitioners about how they mediate the use of digital technologies among children in their care. Some of the following verbs might be helpful in prompting them to speak about how they shape the ways in which children engage with digital technologies, and in turn, what this might mean for the relationship between digital technologies and social interaction (including collaborative creativity, affective alignment and moments of meeting): monitor, manage, intervene, guide, encourage and support.
- Observe children engaged in a collaborative task using a free-flow play app on the iPad (e.g. Puppet Pals or Kids Doodle). Identify moments of collaborative creativity, and moments where collaborative creativity seems to break down. Do the same for affective alignment. How is the digital technology implicated in these moments? Observe children as they engage in a similar task in a non-digital environment. Make comparisons.

FURTHER READING

- Burnett, C. (2014). Investigating pupils' interactions around digital texts: A spatial perspective on the 'classroom-ness' of digital literacy practices in schools. *Educational Review*, 66(2), 192–209.

In this paper, Burnett demonstrates how children's interaction with digital technologies, as part of their literacy practices in a primary school classroom, unfolds in relation to the sociocultural context of the classroom. She develops the concept of 'classroom-ness' to explain how the typical social practices and patterns of the classroom impact on how digital technologies are taken up as part of children's activities, but also how these social practices and patterns are constantly in flux, and are influenced by the presence of digital resources and how children engage with them.

- Edwards, S. (2016). New concepts of play and the problem of technology, digital media and popular-culture integration with play-based learning in early childhood education. *Technology, Pedagogy and Education, 25*(4), 513–532.

In this paper, Edwards offers an understanding of why practitioners often struggle to think about digital play as 'real play' and see it as part of their work in planning and providing for play opportunities. She develops a web-mapping tool that enables practitioners to see how children develop interests and ideas through play in various different contexts and using different resources, including digital technologies and environments. This tool helps practitioners to see the links between digital and non-digital play, rather than seeing them as fundamentally separate phenomena.

- Turkle, S. (2017). *Alone together: Why we expect more from technology and less from each other.* UK: Hachette.

In this book, Turkle presents a fascinating argument about the dangers of technology – particularly social media – in contemporary society when it comes to fostering social connections. Building on a wide range of evidence, she argues that our constant connectedness through the internet means that we are less likely to engage in genuine intimacy with those who we are actually closest to in 'real life'. She puts forwards various suggestions for how we need to develop our everyday practices in order to protect ourselves from the negative impacts of technologies on social interaction. These arguments are applied to family life and ideas about how adults should manage the use of technologies in the lives of the children they care for.

3

PHYSICAL ENGAGEMENT AND SENSORY EXPERIENCE IN DIGITAL PLAY

INTRODUCTION

This chapter focuses on the role of physical engagement and sensory experience in children's digital play. In this chapter we:

- discuss claims that digital technologies are to blame for children's inactive lifestyles, and consider innovative digital technologies designed to get children active in outdoor environments;
- examine debates around the nature of touch in digital play, considering whether sensory experience in digital play can be thought about as impoverished, or whether it is just different from what we are used to;
- explore the relationship between digital technologies and messy-play environments, and how we might create new forms of 'connected play' that bring digital and physical environments into stronger dialogue.

You will have many opportunities to reflect on your own experiences and observations in relation to these issues, and you are also invited to set up play activities and environments for children who you work with or know informally, as a way to explore further how physical engagement and sensory experience unfolds in digital play. The chapter is organised around observations, explanations of theory in relation to these observations, and Research Spotlights that focus on cutting-edge research conducted in this area.

> ## CASE STUDY 3.1
>
> ### JUMPING OVER DIGITAL HURDLES
>
> A 2 year old is playing on the Kinect with his older brother. The Kinect is a device that links users' movements to visual activity on the screen, so gross movement of the body is the main input into the technology. They are both running on the spot and then jumping over hurdles that appear in the game. The toddler roars every so often, showing his excitement. His eyes are wide and intently focused on the screen in front of him. When he successfully jumps over a hurdle in the game, which is marked by a sound in the game, the toddler shouts 'Yes!' then continues to run on the spot. He is panting with the exertion. Every time he jumps over a hurdle he shouts 'Yes!'. His brother wanders off, but the child continues. When he misses a hurdle in the game, he looks towards the adult behind the camera and says, 'Oh no', quietly, but then the game starts again and he continues to run on the spot and jump over the hurdles. When it gets to the end of the game, his older brother wanders back over and gives him a high five.

ACTIVE DIGITAL PLAY

Digital technologies have been blamed for children's inactive lifestyles and the obesity epidemic. Headlines in the popular media suggest that children are staying indoors, glued to their digital devices, rather than engaging in free play outside, and that as a result they are inactive and sedentary, and this is taking a toll on children's health. Some researchers have supported these claims. Research by Clements (2004) compared the lifestyles of mothers when they were children with the lifestyles of their children in contemporary society and found a startling decline in the rates of outdoor play among children. Clements suggested that a key driver of this decline was the rise of digital technologies for children, which acted as a pull factor, tempting children to stay indoors watching television and playing games, rather than going out to play. In Gray's (2011) argument that psychopathological disorders such as anxiety and depression are on the rise as a result of fewer opportunities for free-flow play in childhood, he suggests that a significant factor shaping play is the way that digital technologies can be used by parents and carers to keep children occupied and safe inside.

These fears about digital technologies are based on a perception of digital devices as inevitably screen-based resources that will be used in indoor environments. In response, technology designers have focused on the potentials of digital technology to foster active play, rather than sedentary engagement. There is now a wide variety of digital technologies that involve children's physically active engagement. Popular technologies of this type include the Kinect and the Wii; both devices involve children moving in order to engage with the technology as part of 'exergames'. In the observation above, we see a 2 year old enjoying his participation in an exergame. He is engaged, excited and expending lots of energy. The observation also shows a highly sociable activity, where the game is at the centre of family activity. The observation counters two popular concerns about digital play – that it is sedentary and that it is solitary. When technology designers focus on fostering physical activity, there is no need to blame the obesity epidemic on children's engagement with digital play.

It is not just a question of trying to shoehorn physically active experiences into digital play. Indeed, using the whole body when engaged with digital play has been shown to be a more enjoyable experience for the child or adult engaged in digital play. Bianchi-Berthouze, Kim and Patel (2007) conducted studies of individuals playing the digital game Guitar Hero in two conditions. In the first condition, the participants used their whole bodies to play the game, while in the second condition, they used only their hands. The researchers found that the participants reported higher levels of motivation in the whole body condition. Furthermore, this linked to improved performance in the whole body condition, so that the participants' heightened enjoyment linked to them also doing better within the game. Such studies suggest that active digital play is not just a remedy for unhealthy lifestyles among children, but that it is more appealing to both children and adults than inactive digital play. This might suggest that these forms of digital play will continue to gain in popularity.

Some researchers, however, argue that creating digital play experiences that are active is not enough to counter the problem of unhealthy lifestyles among children. Herrington and Brussoni (2015) argue that it is not as simple as engendering physical activity through digital play, because just as important as physical activity is the environment in which this activity occurs. They suggest that natural outdoor environments are better at affording spontaneous free play, where children feel inspired and open-minded in their play experiences. Certainly, in Gray's (2011) connection between the lack of free play and the rise of psychopathological disorders, the emphasis is on the free nature of the play, rather than it just being physically active. In the observation of the toddler playing with the Kinect, there is limited freedom in the play experience. He is following a game with a clear set of rules and objectives, so his active physical participation is not so embedded in his imaginative exploration as might be the case in free-flow play.

If we place an emphasis on natural environments and free-flow play, different forms of technology come to the fore. We have seen the growth of gaming apps that require you to get out and about in order to have certain experiences or collect digital objects (Boulos & Yang, 2013). Perhaps the most well-known of these apps is Pokemon Go, which involves users exploring the outdoor world and making their way to particular locations in order to collect Pokemon. Another approach has been to augment the outdoor environment, so that free play in a natural landscape prompts particular digital effects and responses. An early example of this was created in the Ambient Wood project (described in Price & Rogers, 2004), where children's outdoor exploration was augmented through sounds and images that drew attention to particular aspects of the external space as it was navigated. Since then, there have been various examples of augmented landscapes and playgrounds, from interactive slides that respond to children's level of activity (Soler-Adillon & Parés, 2009) to robots that move around autonomously and respond to particular play actions from children (Seitinger, 2006).

Despite these experiments with digitally augmented outdoor play, there remains a disconnect between what technologies are capable of and the understanding that free-flow open-ended play opportunities are vital for children's learning and wellbeing. The most exciting examples of digital play within free-flow play have tended to involve relatively simple digital technologies that are easily accessible, such as the use of digital photography, or engagement with simple story-making apps that enable children to take photographs and make audio and video recordings (Canning, Payler, Horsley & Gomez, 2017). In the Research Spotlight, we consider an example of how children might engage with digital photography as part of their outdoor environments, and the advantages that this might bring. Although White's (2015) interest is more in the pedagogical insights that might emerge through children's photography in natural environments, the study demonstrates how digital photography might enhance experiences of play and helps us to consider the points of connection between digital and physical environments that emerge in children's active free-flow play.

RESEARCH SPOTLIGHT

White, E.J. (2015). Seeing is believing? Insights from young children in nature. *International Journal of Early Childhood, 47*(1), 171–188.

AIMS

White explores the role that digital photography might play in enabling practitioners to see what children see in nature-based educational contexts. How might digital photography enable deeper understandings and points of connection between children and adults in relation to play and learning in natural environments? White considers how the 'visual surplus' offered by digital photography might enable children to show adults what is of particular significance to them, and open dialogues that might not otherwise occur.

(Continued)

METHODS

The study followed four preschool children aged 3–4 years old in the same home-based learning environment in New Zealand. For 2 months, the children made weekly outings to local places of natural interest and beauty. Each time they made an outing they carried with them a digital camera on a lanyard around their neck and they were instructed to simply take photographs of whatever they could see. Following each visit, the children each participated in an individual semi-structured interview based around photo elicitation. Looking at the photographs they had taken, they would engage in a conversation with a practitioner about what the photograph meant to them and what it reminded them of. These interviews were audio taped and transcribed and then thematically analysed by a team of practitioner researchers.

FINDINGS

The dialogues between children and practitioners about the children's photographs highlighted the personal and unique meanings of the photographs for each child. As a result of these dialogues, the practitioners described experiencing a greater sense of awareness of the child's perspective, the importance of a child-centred pedagogy and what this should look and feel like in an everyday context. Rather than getting in the way of the children's open-ended inquiry in natural environments, the digital photography enhanced the experience and enabled deeper connections to emerge between the children and adults in the educational settings.

REFLECTION ACTIVITIES

- What examples of active digital play have you observed recently? What examples of outdoor digital play have you observed? What did you observe that you felt worked well and enhanced the children's play experiences? What did you observe that you felt got in the way of an alternative non-digital play experience that would have been more enriching?

- Explore apps that are available for children, that are designed to facilitate connections with outdoor play, for example apps that are about recording the weather, or making stories about adventures outside. Download and use these apps, ideally with one or more children to help you. What did you enjoy about the experience? What did you find difficult or boring?

CASE STUDY 3.2

VICARIOUS TOUCH IN COLLABORATIVE CREATIVE PLAY ON THE IPAD

As part of a research study on how children engage in collaborative creativity through different physical and digital resources, I observed six pairs of children as they engaged in collaborative drawing on the iPad. They used the app Kids Doodle, which allows you to draw with different colours and effects. The children played a game called Squiggle, which involves one of the pair starting the drawing, and the second child in the pair finishing the drawing.

Sometimes, the child who was not engaged in drawing would quietly watch the drawing unfold on the screen, with their hands held together – as though they were stopping themselves from reaching out to engage with the tools themselves. Often though, they would engage in a kind of vicarious touch. As though they were inspired by the touch of the drawer on the screen, they would move their fingers around on the tabletop rapidly, often showing heightened engagement and excitement through their facial expression and widened gaze. They were not in 'their own world' since they were looking at the drawing emerging while engaging in this kind of touch. Instead, they were using vicarious touch to respond to the drawing and signal their interest in the activity. Sometimes, their hands wouldn't move around the tabletop but would dance around in the air.

INTANGIBILITY OR A DIFFERENT KIND OF TOUCH?

Digital technologies respond to touch in particular ways. Some researchers argue that the problem with digital technologies is that they are less responsive in that they do not often give us rich experiences of touch sensation. Mangen (2010) argues that digital play is characterised by intangibility, since digital technologies tend to come in the form of cold hard screens that respond to your touch not through a digital effect, but through a limited physical sensation. When we touch a physical object such as a banana, the touch works in two directions: we touch the banana, but we also experience the touch of the banana – the feel of the texture beneath our fingers. If we squeeze the banana, the touch experience will change in line with how we apply our touch to the object. On the other hand, the responsiveness of digital screens to touch does not respond to the subtleties of pressure – the digital effect will be unaffected. Rich sensory experiences are recognised as a vital part of children's play experiences, so there are concerns that digital play cannot fulfil this need.

Steiner nursery schools take this line of thought to an extreme. Steiner schooling, based on the philosophical insights of Rudolf Steiner, places an emphasis on the need to educate and protect the senses of the child. Steiner practitioners advocate open-ended play experiences for young children, that unfold with the support of natural materials such as wood and hessian. Steiner practitioners are committed to children's creativity and art-making, and suggest that digital technologies get in the way of these experiences because they encourage children to act too quickly without really stopping to consider their sensory engagement. Denmead and Hickman (2012) conducted interviews with adult artists and found a similar scepticism around the potentials of digital technologies in relation to creativity and art-making. The artists argued that it was essential to engage with materials that promote 'slowliness' – this is a kind of slowed-down, thoughtful and exploratory engagement through the physical senses. Digital play might inhibit this slowliness, because, as mentioned earlier, there is not the same responsiveness to the subtleties of the touch interaction. This echoes a concern I found among early years practitioners who I interviewed about digital play: they worried that digital play could never be part of the rich messy experiences that they so strongly associated with early childhood experience (Sakr, 2017).

Careful observations focusing on children's interactions with digital technologies suggest that rather than thinking in terms of sensory impoverishment, it might be more helpful to focus on the specific similarities and differences that arise when we compare digital play with play embedded purely in a physical environment. Research by Crescenzi, Price and Jewitt (2014), looking at the nature of touch when young children do finger painting through the iPad and finger painting on paper, found that there were many similarities in how children approached their touch interactions, as well as some important differences. The researchers found that the children engaged in more touch on the iPad screen as compared with the paper, presumably because the children did not need to remove their finger from their screen in order to re-apply paint. The researchers noted that the finger painting via either set of resources was a thoroughly individual experience. For some children, the touch of the paint on the finger was enjoyable, but for others, they recoiled from this sensory engagement. The screen offered such children a way into the creative activity that felt more manageable for them. This reminds us that we should not simply assume that rich and messy sensory experiences are a part of every young child's life (or that they should be). The context that surrounds each child is more complex than that, and the potentials of digital play in relation to their sensory engagement with the world will depend on the specific factors that shape their use of touch.

Research conducted by Flewitt, Kucirkova and Messer (2014; see Research Spotlight) encourages us to be more open in how we think about the nature of touch in the context of digital technologies. Flewitt et al. suggest that the sensitivity of digital screens – their capacity to respond to even the lightest of touch – can be particularly important for those children who might struggle to apply pressure within their touch, of the kind needed to complete many tasks in the physical environment. Consider, for example, drawing on the iPad using a pencil. Drawing on the iPad can be achieved through an extremely light touch of the fingertip moving across the screen. The line that appears on the iPad will have qualities that have been chosen by the user – the line might be big and bold, or it might be light and fleeting, but these qualities will not be dependent on the level of pressure that the user can apply. On the other hand, when drawing with a pencil, there is a staggering amount of physical dexterity required – from the grip of the pencil, to the application of a fine tip to the paper, to the use of the correct level of pressure in order to achieve the desired effect. Flewitt et al. draw attention to how, in the context of this comparison, the iPad might open literacy and play experiences for children with disabilities that impact on their engagement with touch. Flewitt et al. also highlight the significance of vicarious touch and the need to bring this kind of touch into our thinking around touch, so that we don't only think about those touch interactions that impact directly on the object of focus.

As the observation of collaborative drawing on the iPad above demonstrates, my research suggests that vicarious touch was an essential part of children's digital play with the iPad. Children were drawn to moving their hands around the tabletop or in the air as a response to watching their partner drawing on the iPad. This reminds us that we need to zoom out and consider touch, gesture and sensory experience in general in relation to the whole environment. We cannot just limit our focus and our observational gaze to the specific instances of touch that involve the digital technology directly; touch in the context of digital play is multi-layered and contextual. Paying attention to the many layers of multimodal engagement is supported through a new literacies theoretical approach, which encourages us to think about digital and physical environments as constantly enmeshed and enfolded around one another. When we pay attention to lived experience, we cannot really separate between physical and digital experiences – digital play will always be physical play as well (Burnett, Merchant, Pahl & Rowsell, 2014). Wohlwend (2013, 2015, 2017a) suggests the ideas of the 'literacy playshop' and the 'makerspace' as ways of challenging us to think about how we can bring together resources of all types to support children's play and creativity. Children's play moves across modes and media, involving a wide variety of touch experiences and sensory engagement as a result of this.

RESEARCH SPOTLIGHT

Flewitt, R., Kucirkova, N., & Messer, D. (2014). Touching the virtual, touching the real: iPads and enabling literacy for students experiencing disability. *Australian Journal of Language & Literacy*, 37(2), 107–116.

(Continued)

AIMS

The study aimed to explore how iPads might support literacy learning among students at a school for learners with moderate to complex physical and cognitive disabilities. The researchers had a particular interest in touch and gesture and how these modes of communication might play out in this particular context of engaging with digital technologies. They were interested in how the affordances of the iPad and the particular apps used might enable touch experiences that were embedded in playful literacy learning experiences.

METHODS

The research study centred around a case study of a particular school for 3–18 year olds with special educational needs. The case study involved observations of various learners as they engaged with iPads as part of playful literacy activities. The researchers made video observations and audio-recorded interviews and wrote fieldnotes as part of their investigation. Based on the data, they developed key analytic themes among the research team and amidst ongoing consultation with the ICT coordinator in the school.

FINDINGS

The researchers identified many examples where the iPad appeared to be facilitating a richer and more playful experience of literacy learning for the children in the case study school. They highlighted the touch-sensitivity and responsiveness of the iPad as a key affordance in relation to supporting literacy learning. The touch-sensitivity of the iPad meant that even the smallest touch from a learner using the iPad could create a big visual effect on the screen, which in turn prompted a strong affective and reinforcing response in the learner. So rather than seeing touch as diminished in this digital context, the researchers found that the capacities of touch were augmented for the learners they observed. The study shows how the iPad can open up and heighten the significance of touch in children's learning and play, depending on how we look at the activity and the kinds of learners we are observing.

REFLECTION ACTIVITIES

- Observe a child or children as they engage in digital play, such as doodling on a tablet or phone, engaging with an interactive storybook or playing a game. Watch the video recording and make notes on all the types of touch that they engage with. Do not limit yourself to recording the touch that is applied to the tablet screen – instead record all of the touch interactions that the child engages with. What do you notice about these touch experiences? What are your impressions? Are they limited? Or are they open and expansive? How do they relate to Flewitt et al.'s argument that touch is more complex in digital environments, and should not be thought about as impoverished but rather just as different? Or do you relate the observations more to Mangen's arguments about intangibility: is there a sense of intangibility in the experiences of the children/child you observed?

- Observe children playing together, all huddled around a single device. If you can, video record the observation so that you can watch it back several times in order to answer the following questions. What instances of vicarious touch do you notice (if any)? What is happening in the other modes (e.g. gaze, facial expression, movement) at the same time as the vicarious touch? What role do you think the vicarious touch is fulfilling? How important is the vicarious touch? How do the other children respond to the vicarious touch?

CASE STUDY 3.3

TAKING SELFIES IN THE SAND

I am playing on the living room floor with my 2.5-year-old daughter (Leyla) and my 1-year-old son (Ish). We are playing 'at the beach'. This imaginative play involves playing with a messy mix of rice, lentils and flour, and a collection of spades, buckets and containers that we accumulated during a recent beach holiday. We are pretending that the messy flour mix is our sand. A blue blanket lying on the floor nearby is our sea.

Interested to see what happens when digital play comes into contact with this kind of messy play, I've put my phone on the floor nearby. My phone is in a waterproof plastic wallet that allows you to interact normally with the phone but means it's completely protected from anything spilling on it or messy hands using it.

Leyla and Ish get stuck in straight away with the messy play. Leyla begins to fill different plastic shapes with the flour, using her spade. Ish practises scooping up a bit of the flour mix with the tip of his spade and then flicking it backwards. I gasp whenever it lands on me and this makes him giggle. Sometimes he puts the spade towards his mouth and I have to say 'no, no, no, we don't eat that' and he shakes his head, but still tries to eat it.

I say to Leyla: 'shall we take some selfies at the beach?'. Taking selfies is something that Leyla is often interested in. In the past we've used selfies as an incentive for lots of things including sitting on the potty or the toilet. She likes posing for the selfie,

(Continued)

> saying 'cheeeeeese' and she likes looking back through the photographs. This time, she says 'yes!' enthusiastically to my suggestion, and we take a selfie together. After this though, Leyla is more interested in focusing on the make-believe sand play and she ignores the phone for the rest of the play episode.
>
> Ish drops his spade at one point and begins to use the phone, prodding its screen and swiping it. He does this for a few seconds and then goes back to playing with the spade and buckets. A little later, I say again to Leyla: 'shall we take any more photos?' and she says 'no'. The phone lies discarded on the floor. Both Leyla and Ish are intently engaged in their messy play and Leyla is upset when it is time to tidy up.

MESSY DIGITAL PLAY

As mentioned in the previous section, Karen Wohlwend's idea of the 'playshop' suggests the benefits of bringing together a wide range of resources, both physical and digital, into the same environment, so that children can explore ideas across multiple modes and media. How does this work in practice? On a practical level, the observation above demonstrates that the simplest precautions can make digital technologies compatible with messy play. The inexpensive plastic wallet that I kept the phone in would have allowed the phone to be used alongside water, modelling clay, paint and so on. But the issue is more than just one of practical logistics. A quick scroll through YouTube will demonstrate the extent to which digital play is seen as separate from messy play. While there are many video recordings of children engaging in a wide range of messy-play scenarios, and many video recordings of children engaging in digital play through a plethora of devices, it is difficult to find any recordings that bring these elements together, where the digital technologies are available alongside the materials for messy play. In the videos where this does occur, the focus is on the horror of parents who find their children putting their phones under water from the tap, rather than the potentials of allowing children to explore phones and water simultaneously in their play.

Because of the lack of focus on messy digital play, we know little about the points of connection that children might find between physical and digital environments during free-play episodes. Marsh (2017) applies a list created by Rogers, Scaife, Gabrielli, Smith and Harris (2002) to think about the different points of connection that can link the physical and digital environments in 'connected play'. These are when 1) physical causes lead to physical effects, 2) physical causes lead to digital effects, 3) digital causes lead to digital effects and 4) digital causes lead to physical effects. What are the points of connection in the observation above? The phone has a physical presence, it is part of what gets explored physically, particularly by the 1 year old. Physical interaction with the phone does lead to digital effect, such as the home screen swiping across and the app icons re-sizing, but these are not the focus of the action and this does not lead to any subsequent activity. We take a selfie through the digital phone camera, and this impacts on the physical environment through the set-up of a photograph of us 'at the beach', adding a new dimension to the pretend play experience. But the phone is also a point of resistance, when Leyla does not want to take another selfie, she just wants to continue playing.

As the play moves through the physical–digital environment, it is constantly shifting. Kress (2005a) uses the term 'transduction' to discuss what happens when ideas move across modes and media. Depending on the semiotic resources that we use to express and explore an idea, the meaning-making will be shaped differently. So exploring an idea through drawing is not the same as exploring the idea through writing or play acting. As children move across different modes and media there will be gains and losses (Kress, 2005b), and the idea will develop and adapt each time it's taken up through a different set of resources. Applying Kress' concept of transduction to the observation, this means that pretending to play at the beach by using flour as sand, is different from pretending to play at the beach where the sand is imagined without any particular play prop, and both of these scenarios are different from pretending to play at the beach through a gaming app on a digital tablet. What emerges for the child from these different episodes of play will be particular to the resources that they engaged with during their meaning-making. Through experience, children will develop an implicit awareness of the gains and losses of different play resources and environments. They are unlikely to swap pretend playing at the beach using flour for sand with an app based around playing at the beach. It is more likely that they will experience these two types of play as fundamentally different. One type of play need not be seen as more or less appealing than the other, since they both offer different forms of engagement and experience.

RESEARCH SPOTLIGHT

Marsh, J.A. (2017). The internet of toys: A posthuman and multimodal analysis of connected play. *Teachers College Record*, *119*(15). Available at: http://eprints.whiterose.ac.uk/113557/

AIMS

Marsh explores the nature of play when it unfolds across different environments as a result of toys and apps that connect digital and physical play spaces. Marsh terms this 'connected play' and aims to investigate how popular augmented reality apps that connect an app on a phone or tablet with 'smart toys' (e.g. Lego Fusion) are feeding into the everyday experiences of connected play. In order to investigate this, Marsh adopts a posthumanist philosophy, drawing particularly on the work of Barad, in which the focus is

(Continued)

on the entanglements between humans and non-humans, displacing a traditional focus on human experiences. Marsh draws our attention back towards the materiality of the virtual – rather than thinking about digital environments as being somehow non-physical, she explores through examples of children's connected play how the digital and the physical are constantly intertwined with one another.

METHODS

The paper reports on data from a large study about children's digital play, which involved various stakeholders and both quantitative and qualitative research. However, this particular study focuses on the case study part of the research, which involved six families with young children and data collected through regular visits involving observations, semi-structured interviews with parents and children, and tours of the home. In addition, parents were encouraged from collecting their own video observations of children engaged in digital play between visits from the researchers, and the slightly older children in the study had the option to collect data themselves through a Go-Pro camera. In this paper, Marsh focuses her analysis on just one of the six case studies. She focuses on a girl called Amy aged 2 years and 11 months and her experiences of connected play. Marsh chose to focus on Amy because she showed more involvement than the other children in experiences of connected play, since she owned her own Samsung Tab, used her parents' iPad regularly, and had a range of 'smart toys' to play with. In this paper, Marsh describes two particular play episodes: in the first, Amy is feeding her toy Furby through the Furby app; in the second episode, Amy is playing with her PAW Patrol toys, and using the music in the PAW Patrol App as part of the multimodal play experience, providing dramatic tension to her imaginary play. Both of these episodes are analysed through a close multimodal interaction analysis, which involves mapping the various modes (e.g. gaze, body position, gesture, touch and so on) involved in the play episode, and how these relate to the different resources available.

FINDINGS

The episodes selected by Marsh for careful analysis demonstrate the constant back-and-forth across the physical and the digital environments. Marsh offers the example of when the toy Furby is encouraged by the Furby app to use the toilet. In the context of the app, Amy then flushes the visual toilet on the screen. While doing this though, she pretends that she has faeces on her hands, pretending that she needs to get it off her and that she is disgusted. This example clearly demonstrates the connectedness of the play: the 'constant flow between domains' (p. 26). To help us to get to grips with the various ways in which connected play can flow and move between domains, Marsh cites Rogers et al. (2002) in explaining all of the links and points of connection that we need to remain aware of: physical action prompts physical effect; physical action causes digital effect; digital action creates digital effect; and digital action creates physical effect.

> Amy rubbing the 'faeces' off her hands shows another layer of complexity in this model; what does this count as? Is it a digital cause with a physical effect, or is this too deterministic? Amy's imagination seems to play a vital role in enabling new points of connections across the domains, and we need to be open to the ways in which play will transgress the physical–digital boundaries that we might expect to find in connected play.

REFLECTION ACTIVITIES

- Have you seen any examples of children engaging in messy digital play, where digital technologies are brought into contact with water, sand, paint, etc.? If so, what did it involve? How did the children move between the different resources that they had access to? What were the points of connection between the physical and the digital environments?

- It is possible that you have never observed examples of messy digital play occurring naturally. In my experience, it is a rare thing! So we need to think about the barriers that are inhibiting messy digital play from unfolding. What are the barriers to messy digital play in the lives of the children you work/live with or know informally? What stops messy digital play from happening?

- Experiment with messy digital play among children who you work with or know informally. Think about the physical materials that you want to use, and then the digital technologies and apps that might find points of connection with the physical materials. For example, you might set up water play with tablets nearby (with waterproof protective covers on) set up with apps about exploring under the sea. Video record the children as they engage in the play episode over a prolonged period. Watch the video recording and make notes on the physical–digital points of connection that emerge.

CHAPTER SUMMARY

- While digital technologies have been blamed for the rise in obesity among children, designers of digital technologies have shown that digital play can facilitate physical activity among children and even encourage them to get outdoors and explore the natural environment.

- Some researchers and practitioners suggest that digital play is impoverished in terms of sensory experience when we compare it with play that occurs in a purely physical environment.

(Continued)

- Other researchers, however, argue that it is more helpful to think about touch within digital play as different rather than impoverished. Digital devices can be particularly responsive to touch, and this can be helpful for children who have disabilities that limit the subtleties of their engagement with touch. Another important aspect of digital play is the significance of vicarious touch, whereby children engage in gestures that mimic the touch interactions they would engage with were they using the device directly.

- Digital technologies are not typically situated in a context of messy play. This is partly practical (because of the need to protect the technology from damage), but the real barrier here seems to be one of association – we don't associate digital play with messy materials such as sand, water, flour and modelling clay, and as a result, we stop these resources from coming into contact with one another.

- In a new literacies approach, the digital and physical environments are conceptualised as constantly mixed up with one another. When we observe 'connected play', we become more aware of how digital and physical actions relate to one another in constantly shifting ways.

RESEARCH ACTIVITIES

- Interview practitioners about the activities they set up for children, that relate to digital play being 1) active, 2) happening in natural environments and 3) happening as part of messy play and rich sensory experiences. Interview practitioners about the things that facilitate these types of digital play activities, but also about the barriers that make it difficult to involve digital resources in these play contexts. As part of the interview, share some of the examples in this chapter with the practitioner of how digital play can be more active and messy and can happen outdoors. What are their responses to these scenarios? Do they feel inspired? Are they sceptical? What ideas come to mind, building on the ideas presented here?

- Set up a series of observations that take digital play into contexts in which we wouldn't expect to find it: rich sensory contexts. Video record the observations. Observe the flow of the play across different contexts, and different resources. Map the interactions. As a starting point, use Marsh's (2017) analysis of connected play, and her breakdown (building on Rogers et al., 2002) of cause–effect relationships across digital–physical boundaries. What surprises you about the observation? Did you feel that the digital technologies added something? What did they bring?

FURTHER READING

- Giddings, S. (2014). *Gameworlds: Virtual media and children's everyday play*. London: Bloomsbury.

In this book, Giddings explores the relationships between children's digital play and other forms of their play in everyday contexts. He focuses on the embodied nature of digital play, pushing against a conceptualisation of digital play as somehow immaterial and not real. Giddings argues that when we look closely at how digital play crosses over into other forms of play, we become more aware of the highly physicalised nature of all play engagement, including play that unfolds in digital environments.

- Mangen, A. (2010). Point and click: Theoretical and phenomenological reflections on the digitization of early childhood education. *Contemporary Issues in Early Childhood*, 11(4), 415–431.

In this paper, Mangen reflects on the role of digital technologies in preschool environments, drawing on research from cognitive neuroscience, media psychology and phenomenology. Mangen focuses particularly on the issue of tangibility/intangibility. This issue draws attention to the distinct nature of the cause–effect relationships that govern engagement in digital environments as opposed to activity unfolding in the actual world. Mangen argues that this leads to a fundamentally different experience for children when they engage in play through digital as opposed to physical environments, and that this needs to be a primary focus when we think about the role of digital play in early years environments.

- Marsh, J., Plowman, L., Yamada-Rice, D., Bishop, J., & Scott, F. (2016). Digital play: A new classification. *Early Years*, 36(3), 242–253.

Marsh et al. (2016) report on a study of children's use of apps at home and how different apps can shape play and creativity among children. The researchers focus particularly on the role of transgression in digital play, that is, the creative ways in which children use apps not as they were intended to be used by the designers.

4
DIGITAL TECHNOLOGIES AND OUTDOOR PLAY

INTRODUCTION

This chapter focuses on the relationship between digital technologies and outdoor play. The chapter:

- evaluates evidence that digital play is to blame for the decline of outdoor play among children in the West;
- presents the debate between those who see digital technologies as detracting from the fulfilment of children's deepest play instincts, based on a desire to connect directly with nature, and those who suggest that technology has always been a part of the human relationship with nature and that digital play is simply an extension of this;
- examines material and social factors that typically prevent digital play from unfolding in the outdoor environment of early years learning environments, and considers how we can 'shake up' these environments in order to enable outdoor digital play.

In fulfilling these aims, you are invited to consider the experiences that you see around you in your everyday life, as well as connect the theoretical ideas with headlines from popular media, observations of children playing outside and practitioner ideas about creating apps designed to facilitate outdoor exploration and play. The Research Spotlight sections focus on recent findings around trends in children's play habits, as well as ideas from digital designers about how to support outdoor play through innovative digital play props.

> ## CASE STUDY 4.1
>
> ### 'THREE-QUARTERS OF UK CHILDREN SPEND LESS TIME OUTDOORS THAN PRISON INMATES' (CARRINGTON, 2016)
>
> A survey conducted in 2016 asked 2000 parents to document the amount of outdoor play their children (aged between 5 and 12 years old) were doing. The survey found that 74% of the children were spending less than 60 minutes in an average day playing outside. According to United Nations guidelines, prisoners should spend at least 1 hour a day engaged in outdoor exercise, leading the popular media to make the uncomfortable comparison between children in the UK and prisoners. The survey also found that this group of children spent twice as long playing on screens as playing outdoors.

ARE DIGITAL TECHNOLOGIES TO BLAME FOR THE DECLINE IN OUTDOOR PLAY?

A popular concern in the UK, and across industrialised countries around the world, is the decline of free outdoor play among children. Many headlines, including the one above, focus on the lack of opportunities that children have to play outside in an unstructured way. Commentators worry that children have no time and freedom in their lives to run around outside, make dens or climb trees. Research studies support this concern. For example, a study by Clements (2004) asked 80 mothers to compare their memories of playing in childhood with the experiences of their own children, and showed a marked difference in the amount of time engaged in outdoor play, across just a single generation. Tandon, Zhou and Christakis (2012) found that just 51% of a sample of more than 8000 children went outside for play time with their parents at least once a day. Gray (2011) argues that the decline of free play, including outdoor play, is having severe negative consequences for the mental health of children, young people and the adults they become. Gray suggests that without opportunities for free play, children grow up without a strong sense of who they are and what they are interested in, separate from others and extrinsic rewards. This leads, he argues, to psychopathological disorders such as anxiety and depression, which appear to have risen over the last 50 years in the Western world as much as free-play opportunities have declined. Both Clements (2004) and Gray (2011), as well as others such as Skår and Krogh (2009), suggest that digital technologies are at least partly to blame for the decline of outdoor free play. They argue that children are less inclined to go outdoors because digital play has such an important role in their leisure time, and parents encourage children to stay indoors and play on digital devices because they are worried about the safety and security of their children in outdoor environments.

As a result of surveys and research studies such as these, outdoor play and digital play are often positioned as opposing one another. In his foundational book about evolutionary playwork, Bob Hughes (2011), argues vehemently that the rise of digital technology has had a fundamental part to play not just in the decline of outdoor play, but in the reduction of opportunities for children to express their deepest play instincts. From a playwork perspective, nature play involving the elements, animals and wild landscapes is a fundamental part of the human desire to be in touch and make sense of the environment around us. Hughes argues that humans have not changed much from the point at which our species came into existence, and it is this prehistorical landscape and life to which our deepest play instincts as children actually respond. Children are therefore most fulfilled when they are playing in the same way as children who would have lived tens of thousands of years ago – unfettered by digital technologies. Hughes describes digital play as a 'technological vice into which their [children's] heads are being forced' (p. 365) – a factor in contemporary society that grips children in a harmful way and prevents them from getting the outdoor play they require.

While Hughes' passionate arguments resonate among many practitioners, the research shows a more nuanced picture regarding the decline in outdoor play. No research study suggests that if we simply removed digital technologies, children's lives would instantly involve a much larger degree of outdoor play. Instead, the research points towards a variety of factors that impact on how and where children spend their time. Most parents are in fact positive about outdoor play and believe it to be vital for children's development and wellbeing, but concerns about safety (as a result of strangers and traffic) remain at the forefront of their minds and can stop them from letting their children out to play unless they are there to supervise (O'Brien & Smith, 2002; Veitch, Bagley, Ball & Salmon, 2006; Witten, Kearns, Carroll, Asiasiga & Tava'e, 2013). When children are asked, research suggests that it isn't the lure of digital play that gets in the way of outdoor play but other social factors, including the risk of being bullied by older children during unsupervised outdoor play time, and the practical limitations of going outside in rainy weather. Since families in contemporary society typically involve two working parents and a range of organised activities for children – some of them designed to help them 'get ahead' academically – there may simply be very little time where parents and children can get out of the house together and enjoy free outdoor play. It is more than just the practical difficulties. There is an emotional dimension of this set-up to consider. Parents who spend so much of their time at work might feel that letting their children get on with 'free play' outdoors is a wasted opportunity to be together in the context of explicitly purposeful activity. Alternatively, children might state the desire to be with their parents and engage in something together; many parents are not experienced free players, and may feel more comfortable 'doing' something in particular with their children rather than just going to a wide green space and seeing what happens. In this wider 'ecology of play' (Dezuanni & Knight, 2015), digital play may be something that children take up and do more of, but it does not make sense to simply place outdoor play and digital play in stark opposition with each other. Even naming these as 'types' of play might be unhelpful, since it suggests that outdoor digital play is not possible, when – as we shall see in the following section of the chapter – it absolutely is.

RESEARCH SPOTLIGHT

Tandon, P.S., Zhou, C., & Christakis, D.A. (2012). Frequency of parent-supervised outdoor play of US preschool-aged children. *Archives of Pediatrics & Adolescent Medicine*, *166*(8), 707–712.

AIMS

This research study focused on the parent-reported frequency of outdoor play among preschool children in the US. The researchers sought to understand how different social and cultural factors would impact on the frequency of parent-supervised outdoor play sessions. These factors included whether parents were working or looking after children in the home, the sex and ethnicity of the child, the parents' engagement with exercise themselves, household income, parental perceptions regarding safety of the neighbourhood and the amount of television watched by their children. For our interest in digital technologies and outdoor play, the last factor is the most vital – does screen time negatively correlate with time engaged in outdoor play?

METHODS

The research involved structured interview responses from 8950 parents of preschool children. The data were taken from the Early Childhood Longitudinal Study Birth Cohort, which followed a total of more than 10,000 children who were born in 2001 in the US. The parents were asked how often they had been outside with their children engaged in play over the last year, and they rated this – so the focus was on parent-supervised outdoor play, rather than outdoor play more generally, and we need to remain aware of this. Statistical analysis was used to determine whether the different social and cultural factors mentioned above are related to the frequency of parent-supervised outdoor play.

FINDINGS

About half of the children asked about did not have daily parent-supervised outdoor play. As mentioned above, this does not mean that they did not engage in daily outdoor play, since this may have been made possible through extended family or a childcare provider. The researchers found through the statistical analysis that girls were significantly less

(Continued)

likely to engage in parent-supervised outdoor play than boys. On the other hand, household income, perceptions of neighbourhood safety and screen time did not significantly correlate with the frequency of parent-supervised outdoor play. The average screen time among the preschoolers was 3.78 hours – higher than other studies have suggested, but this did not seem to impact on whether or not children were going outdoors with their parents frequently, suggesting that digital technologies including television cannot be blamed for the suggested decline in outdoor play.

REFLECTION ACTIVITIES

- Think about a child who you know – a family member perhaps, or the child of a friend. Speak to them about their opportunities for outdoor play. How much outdoor play do they do? When do they get to do outdoor play? What are some of the limiting factors that impact on how much outdoor play they can do? Does digital technology come up in this conversation? If so, how? Make notes on your conversation and reflect on what it suggests about the relationship between outdoor play and digital play.

- Speak to the child's parents/carers if possible. What are some of the barriers, as well as potentially the enabling factors, that shape their child's outdoor play experiences? Again, does digital technology come up in the conversation as a factor? What other factors shape outdoor play experiences for children in contemporary society?

CASE STUDY 4.2

WALKING HOME IN THE DARK

It's around 8pm on a Friday night. After dinner at her grandparents' house, Leyla (2½ years old) is walking back home across the park. It's a short walk, less than 10 minutes, but part of the journey is in almost complete darkness, with little light filtering into the park, particularly along one part of the path. Leyla is with her mother, father and baby brother, who is in the pushchair. Leyla says 'we need a torch!', and her father takes out his phone and uses the 'torch' setting to light up the path ahead. Leyla is delighted with the torch and the way that the light makes shadows across the path. She runs in and out of the light, pretending that she is chasing her shadow. She is fascinated to see how her shadow grows and diminishes in size. She looks for other shadows: 'Mummy, where's your shadow?', and I explain that I'm not in front of the light, and so I don't have a shadow. As Leyla dances in and out of the light, making her shadow disappear and reappear, move around and change size, her baby brother laughs and claps his hands.

TECHNOLOGY HAS ALWAYS BEEN A PART OF NATURE PLAY

Hughes (2011) argues vehemently that digital technologies are getting in the way of children's deepest play instincts. He suggests that play, as a tool for the development of essential survival skills, emerged in the process of evolution and is therefore responsive to the most basic needs and instincts of humans – the same needs and instincts that we had tens of thousands of years ago. If play today is to fulfil children's needs, it needs to be a similar type of play that children have the opportunity to do. As a result, Hughes places the emphasis on play in outdoor environments, a kind of animal play where children master the natural environment, building dens, making pathways, climbing trees and so on. In this kind of play, the natural elements are of utmost importance. Play is a way of coming to know about mud, water, fire and so on. Digital technologies and the underlying logic of digital environments have no place in this kind of natural interaction.

However, the opposition that Hughes constructs between nature and technology can be countered by arguments that suggest that technology has always played a part in humans' relationships with nature. Just as the human species has always been deeply concerned with mastery over natural environments, creating technologies that support this process has been vital to the evolution of humans. In his theory of originary technicity, Stiegler (1998) argues that humans have always been technological – they have always incorporated non-human technologies into the practical everyday realities of being a human, and 'technicity' has therefore become a part of what it means to be human. Making fire, for example, depends on a technology, if we think about technology as a set of tools and skills, actions and artefacts coupled together that allow new forms of human–environment interaction to unfold. So, contrary to Hughes (2011), we can argue that engagement with digital technologies is a continuation of this evolutionary history rather than a damaging divergence from what it means to be human.

One way to think about humans' relationship with technology is through the concept of 'distributed cognition' (Cole & Engeström, 1993). Cognition is the mental processes that are required for all that we do – the thinking, the imagining, the believing, the planning and so on. We associate cognition with our minds and therefore see these processes as happening within us. However, the concept of distributed cognition highlights the extent to which humans offload many of these processes to external tools. Take as an example using a calculator. When we use a calculator we offload the mental processes involved in making mathematical calculations. This is helpful because when we offload cognitive processes in this way, we free up cognition for other processes, meaning that overall, we can achieve much more. So it makes sense to want to incorporate technologies, whether digital or non-digital, into what we do in order to expand our capabilities.

When we consider children's digital play from a distributed cognition perspective, we start to look for the ways in which the digital technologies are expanding children's potential for creativity and innovation in the outdoor environment, their mastery of nature, rather than seeing digital technologies as getting in the way of this. Hughes argues that digital technologies detract from immersion in the natural environment, but if we think about pathfinding using an app such as Google Maps, which can read off directions to you from a device in your pocket, there is actually more opportunity for the individual or group to engage actively with the environment around them. Rather than having to look down at a map and focus a lot of attention on the map, the individuals can look around them, noticing new things in the surrounding environment and their hands are free to interact through touch with whatever they are curious about. Maps, compasses, torches (as in the observation above) are non-digital technologies that are strongly associated with interactions with the natural outdoor environment. These technologies are all available in a digital format that extends their capabilities, offloading cognitive processes onto external tools to an even greater extent. From this perspective therefore, digital outdoor play is an inevitable advancement and demonstration of humans' instincts.

RESEARCH SPOTLIGHT

Hitron, T., David, I., Ofer, N., Grishko, A., Wald, I.Y., Erel, H., & Zuckerman, O. (2018). Digital outdoor play: Benefits and risks from an interaction design perspective. In *Proceedings of the 2018 Computer–Human Interaction (CHI) Conference on Human Factors in Computing Systems* (p. 284). ACM Digital Library.

AIMS

The researchers aimed to investigate how digital technologies integrated into the outdoor play experience can impact on the benefits of outdoor play, including social interaction, creative thinking and physical activity. The research study builds on human–computer interaction design principles of 'Head Up Games' (HUG), which are digital games that are designed for use in outdoor environments, and are intended to keep the player's head up and actively engaged with the outdoor environment and immediate social interaction. This is related to the approach of 'transparent technology', which is the intention to seamlessly integrate digital technologies into everyday activities. In practice, this means using existing outdoor play objects as inspiration for the design of digital play objects.

METHODS

The researcher-designers present their digital play prop design, which takes the form of a 'stick' that prompts digital feedback effects through physical activity with it, for example lighting up when it is thrown or shaken in a particular way. The researchers observed 48 children aged 8–12 as they interacted with the stick in 16 groups of 3 individuals. Each group was observed in two conditions: a non-digital condition in which the stick was 'just' a stick, and the digital condition in which the stick's digital feedback was switched on, and shaking and throwing would lead to particular sound and visual effects. All sessions were video recorded. The video observations were coded for social interaction, physical activity and creative rule generation (i.e. children inventing their own rules for games) by two coders. Statistical comparisons were made between the digital and non-digital conditions.

FINDINGS

The observations suggested that social collaboration and rule generation were negatively impacted in the digital condition. When the digital feedback of the 'stick' was turned on, children were less likely to work together and less likely to invent their own rules for playing with the prop. On the other hand, levels of physical activity and social competition were not different between the digital and the non-digital conditions. Within the digital condition, particular design features were found to influence social interaction. For example, how much digital feedback was given to the children at particular points in the game impacted on whether they were more likely to adopt a collaborative or competitive game-playing stance. The results suggest that social interaction, physical activity and rule generation can be negatively impacted by incorporating digital play props into outdoor play, but that this also depends on the particular design features of the digital play props. Designers need to be careful to create digital play props for outdoor environments that bring children together in their play and offer opportunities for creative engagement, rather than simply creating the technologies that offer the most visual and auditory stimulation.

REFLECTION ACTIVITIES

- Some researchers argue that digital technologies get in the way of children's deepest play instincts in relation to outdoor play. Others suggest that technologies have always been part of outdoor play, and that digital technologies are simply the next step in this natural relationship. What do you think? Which argument are you most convinced by? Which relates most strongly to your everyday experiences of play, digital engagement and nature?

- Think about different outdoor activities that are popular among children and families, for example orienteering, camping, birdwatching and so on. For each of these activities, map the technologies (digital and non-digital) that you associate with the activity (e.g. compass, map, binoculars).

- Having mapped the non-digital technologies that are associated with these activities, we can think about the potential role of digital technologies in the activity.

(Continued)

Digital technology may be able to take over some of the functions of non-digital technology, such as a compass app on a smartphone that behaves the same as a non-digital compass would behave. Alternatively, digital technologies might enhance the functions of the non-digital technology, for example, a 'maps' app on a smartphone enables a different kind of map-reading and pathfinding from engagement with a traditional map. Use these potential links between the non-digital and digital technologies (same function or extended function) as a way of opening up the possibilities for digital technologies in relation to outdoor play and exploration. Which non-digital technologies could be replaced by an app on a smartphone? Can you think of potential digital technologies that would extend what is possible through the use of non-digital tools (e.g. a torch app that changes the colour of the light depending on movement of the user)?

- Once you have ideas about the potential functions that digital technologies might be able to support within an outdoor play context, you can look at different apps that are available that relate to these functions. Document what you find. There is no need to purchase the apps; instead, jot down some notes about each app and the functions it is advertised as fulfilling. Are you surprised by the list you develop? Do the potentials of digital technologies in outdoor activities go beyond what you had expected? Which of the apps that you came across might be worth trying out with children as part of play?

CASE STUDY 4.3

PRACTITIONERS BRAINSTORMING AN APP FOR OUTDOOR PLAY AND EXPLORATION

In June 2018, Middlesex University hosted a workshop for 20 practitioners in early years education to explore apps that are available for young children and to explore collaboratively the design of new apps. One group of five practitioners worked together brainstorming a new app that would be used by 3–8 year olds to enhance their outdoor exploration and play. The app would support children to record what they find during their outdoor exploration – taking photographs of plants, minibeasts and trees, and making recordings of different natural sounds in the environment, such as birdsong. The app would help the children to identify what they found, enabling access to a catalogue of trees, plants, bird sounds, animals and so on. Children could use the app as a portal to finding out more from online sources, for example videos about biological processes. They could also record what they find in more creative ways, for example making use of the time lapse tool to extend their investigations. The device would include an embedded magnifying glass, compass, torch and other helpful tools for investigation of outdoor environments. The practitioners' ideas for an app are so compelling because their ideas start with the genuine excitement that surrounds children's outdoor exploration. The functions of the app feed off the activities that children are already interested in doing outside – finding plants and animals, listening and responding to the sounds around them, and trying to find out more about the world that surrounds them.

SOCIAL AND MATERIAL CONSTRAINTS AROUND PLAY OUTDOORS WITH DIGITAL TECHNOLOGIES

Practitioners often use the term 'free-flow' to talk about the environments for play that they create. The word suggests that children are free to move their ideas and activities between different spaces, drawing on a diverse range of resources to support their play as it evolves. For example, we would expect that a child in a free-flow environment would have the opportunity to take ideas from the 'blocks area' onto the drawing table, and that resources from these two areas could be mixed and matched as part of the child's creative and playful engagement. While free-flow environments are an exciting aspiration, in reality there are lots of ways in which children's movement, both physically and mentally, is constrained within their everyday play environments. For example, practitioners or parents might become frustrated with them when they take resources from one part of the environment and put them into another part of the environment.

As well as adults' social reactions, children will respond – even unconsciously – to the physical boundaries that can exist around different play spaces. For example, Sakr and Scollan (2019) draw attention to the physical cues that surround the interactive whiteboard (IWB) in a supposedly free-flow learning environment in a reception classroom (4–5 year olds) of a UK school, and impact on how children move in and out of the space that surrounds the IWB. These physical cues include a sand-timer that is placed next to the IWB and was taken by the children to indicate that they needed to be careful about not taking 'too long' with the resources, and that it was appropriate to queue for the resources, waiting for their turn (see Chapter 2). While this response of the children to the sand-timer cue meant that the environment was perhaps more 'ordered' around the IWB, opportunities for collaborative creativity, where children could work together and interact more fluidly with the resources, were effectively shut down. Thus, in even the most apparently free educational environments, we need to be aware that particular social and material constraints will exist around different resources that are available.

Around digital technologies in the learning environment, the social and material constraints are likely to be particularly prominent as a result of the concern among practitioners that digital technologies are scarce, fragile, strongly desired and therefore likely to be part of social conflict between children.

In inspiring digital outdoor play, bringing together the benefits of children exploring outside with the potentials of digital technologies, we will need to tackle stubborn social and material constraints around resources that stem from practitioners' scepticism concerning integrating digital technologies into children's everyday educational experiences (Edwards, 2016). For example, the perception that digital devices are fragile and need to be protected will negatively impact on the potential for children to take these devices outdoors and use them freely without supervision. However, protective cases and waterproof pockets can make devices suitable as part of even the wettest, muddiest play. The perception that digital devices means 'heads down' will lead practitioners keen on children's interactions with the natural environment to prevent children from taking the devices outside, as they attempt to safeguard children's immersion in the outdoor landscape. However, as previously mentioned in this chapter, some digital devices are designed specifically to enable 'heads up' interaction – helping children to tune into the natural environment rather than tune out of it (Hitron et al., 2018). Thus, integrating digital technologies into early years pedagogy – and perhaps particularly into the focus on outdoor play and exploration – requires confidence and the willingness to explore and experiment. Previous research focusing on practitioners' attitudes and interactions around digital technologies suggest that this is a weakness among some practitioners, who prefer to stick to what they know works and refrain from engaging with digital technologies that they worry will 'ruin' the experiences that they came into early years education to observe and support (Plowman et al., 2010; Edwards, 2016).

YOUR IMPRESSIONS OF DIGITAL PLAY IN AN OUTDOOR ENVIRONMENT

Take the image below (Figure 4.1), which shows a young child playing on a digital tablet while in the garden. What are your impressions of the activity? Do you think the child is getting the most out of the outdoor environment? How might the digital engagement support and enable their connection to nature in the outdoor environment? How might it inhibit the kind of outdoor play you would most like to see young children doing? How might the experience be different if another digital device were being used as part of the experience? How are the affordances of this particular device shaping both the kind of outdoor play that the child can do and how digital play might be a part of this?

Figure 4.1 Digital engagement in the outdoor environment

RESEARCH SPOTLIGHT

Schilhab, T. (2017) Impact of iPads on break-time in primary schools – a Danish context. *Oxford Review of Education*, 43(3), 261–275.

AIMS

This researcher sought to find out more about the impact of iPads being available to children during break-times in school. This question came about as a result of the one pupil to one device policy introduced in Copenhagen, which meant that children in the city would potentially have access to an iPad in school all day long. The researchers were particularly interested to see whether the presence of iPads during break-time would lead to a decline in outdoor, highly social forms of play – such as organised games of 'tag' or 'bulldog'.

METHODS

The researcher interviewed a range of children and practitioners about the impact of the new policy over the course of an academic year. Their interviews included ten children from three different schools across Copenhagen, aged between 7 and 16 years old. They conducted interviews and focus groups with a total of 30 practitioners from different

(Continued)

settings. The analysis of the interview responses organises the findings according to three different age groups, since the change was managed and manifested differently depending on the age group of the children.

FINDINGS

For the youngest children, aged 7–11 years old, soon after the introduction of the one device per child policy, practitioners implemented a ban in most schools in the city involving the use of iPads during break-time. The ban came about as a result of severe concerns among parents that because of novelty value, children would stay on the iPads all day, and that this would negatively impact on the levels of physical activity they engaged with over the course of the day. For the older children in the study, who were allowed by the teachers to access the iPads if they wanted to during break-time, the children discussed with the researcher some instances where the iPads did seem to get in the way of bigger collaborative play episodes. Organising group games became more difficult because individual children were torn between participating in these social play episodes or playing on their iPad with the recreational time that was left before classes resumed.

REFLECTION ACTIVITIES

- Think about a setting where you have been based either in a voluntary or paid capacity. What are the factors that impact on the potential for digital technologies to be part of outdoor play in this setting? Organise these factors into those that are about the material properties of the devices (e.g. the physical fragility of the technologies and concerns around them being damaged if they are integrated into children's boisterous outdoor play) and social associations and expectations (e.g. the perception that children need outdoor play in order to 'get away' from digital play, thereby positioning the two 'types' of play in opposition to each other).

- Sakr and Scollan (2019) invite practitioners to 'shake up' and disrupt the typical boundaries that surround digital technologies in a free-flow learning environment. This involves trying out social experiments within the setting and seeing what happens – for example, Rose and Whitty (2010) saw what happened when they removed all clocks and watches from one early years setting. What experiments would you set up in a setting to see how the integration of digital technologies into outdoor play might unfold differently? If you have access to a setting, might there be the opportunity to implement this kind of experiment? This might be something you want to do as part of a larger research project or dissertation.

CHAPTER SUMMARY

- Research demonstrates that the frequency of outdoor play among children in the West is declining. While popular headlines and some theorists blame this phenomenon on the rise of digital play, research with parents and children suggests that the reasons underlying the decline of outdoor play are actually more complex, comprising a bundle of factors including the perception of neighbourhood safety and the rise of structured activities that children do outside of their schooling.

- When we place digital play and outdoor play in opposition to each other, we are likely to confound the problem because we make it difficult to engage in possibility thinking about the future of digital outdoor play. So it might be unhelpful to describe outdoor play and digital play as two separate 'types' of play.

- While Hughes (2011) argues that digital technologies detract from the fulfilment of children's deepest play instincts, Stiegler's (1998) theory of originary technicity suggests that humans (and therefore the human instinct to play) have always embraced technological advancement, and digital technologies are an inevitable advancement of this orientation towards technology as part of everyday life.

- Even in a free-flow learning environment, material and social factors will constrain how play flows across spaces and resources. Research suggests that practitioners' association of digital technologies with fragility, scarcity and solitude will impact negatively on their proactive provision of opportunities for children to take up digital play in creative and varied ways, including as part of outdoor play. Thus, there is an urgent need for practitioners to develop the confidence and desire to experiment with the routines, habits and material organisation of the environment in order to open up new opportunities for digital play to bring children closer to nature and outdoor exploration.

RESEARCH ACTIVITIES

- Host a focus group for children to investigate further the decline of outdoor play and explore in more depth the reasons for this. What are some of the reasons for children not engaging in outdoor play more often? How do children see outdoor play? What are their associations? Ask the children about their perceptions of digital technologies, and the extent to which these are to blame for the decline of outdoor play. You might want to extend this research project by also interviewing teachers and/or parents, asking similar questions about the barriers that are limiting children's outdoor play.

- With children, use some apps that are designed for outdoor play and exploration. These might be basic functions available on a smartphone, such as the torch, compass,

(Continued)

or maps app, or these might be more developed functions, such as apps that enable children to record their experiences outdoors through photographs, videos and audio recordings. Create an observation of children using these different digital tools. What do you notice about their engagement? How does the digital technology mediate their engagement with the outdoor environment? Do they seem to move closer to or further away from interactions with nature?

- Conduct observations over the course of a day based on interactions that unfold around the transition space between indoors and outdoors in a free-flow learning environment. Witness the movement of resources across this divide. Which resources are allowed to move between the indoor and outdoor environment? Which resources are prohibited from moving across the divide? How do digital technologies feature in this? Are any digital technologies allowed to go outside? If so, which ones? What constraints are placed on the digital resources and where they are allowed to be engaged with?

FURTHER READING

- Hughes, B. (2011) *Evolutionary playwork* (2nd ed.). London: Routledge.

Bob Hughes presents his theory of evolutionary playwork, which is based on the idea that play is a deep instinct primarily there to enhance the survival skills of children. Hughes argues that digital technologies are detracting from the fulfilment of children's deepest play instincts, which centre around unfettered interactions with nature and the natural elements of mud, water, fire, etc.

- Sakr, M. & Scollan, A. (2019) The screen and the sand-timer: The integration of the interactive whiteboard into an early years free-flow learning environment. *Journal of Early Childhood Research*. Available at: https://doi.org/10.1177/1476718X19851538

Sakr and Scollan explore how the social and material conditions of an early years learning environment shape how children engage with the Interactive Whiteboard (IWB) during free-flow activity time. Observations of how children enter and exit from the space around the IWB show how the way the practitioners set up the environment impact on the way that the children engage in digital play. While these social and material conditions relate to the indoor learning environment, they can give us 'food for thought' in relation to thinking about the flow of digital play across different parts of the learning environment and how this flow is facilitated or constrained through the set-up of the environment.

- Soute, I., Markopoulos, P., & Magielse, R. (2010). Head Up Games: Combining the best of both worlds by merging traditional and digital play. *Personal and Ubiquitous Computing, 14*(5), 435–444.

Soute et al. present the principles of Head Up Games, which are digital play props designed to strengthen the connections that individuals have to the 'real' material and social environment around them, rather than encouraging them to disappear into a digital world that seems to be divorced from the immediate physical environment.

5
IMAGINATION AND CREATIVITY IN DIGITAL ENVIRONMENTS

INTRODUCTION

In this chapter, we consider the relationship between children's imagination and their play in digital environments. The chapter:

- conceptualises imagination and creativity through the theory of possibility thinking, examining how the different features of possibility thinking may be impacted in digital play environments;
- examines debates around originality and imagination that pre-date the introduction of digital play environments, and introduces the concepts of 'remix' and 'mash-up' as ways of thinking about imagination in digital play;
- introduces the notion of 'transgressive play', which is children's play that goes beyond the expectations of the designers of digital play environments, and therefore constitutes a positive demonstration of the imagination that children can bring to digital play.

The chapter invites you to conduct your own observations in relation to these issues, as well as reflecting on your own experiences and opinions. The chapter is organised around observations of children in different digital play environments – two observations of children engaged in creative play in digital environments, and one observation of a child interacting with the conversational agent Alexa. These observations are used as a starting point for discussing key theories that help us to make sense of the relationship between imagination and digital play. Research Spotlight sections offer an overview of key pieces of cutting-edge research that help us to develop a deeper understanding of how children bring their imagination to bear in particular situations of digital play.

CASE STUDY 5.1

COLLABORATIVE DRAWING ON THE IPAD: WHAT COULD IT BE?

Two children (aged 6 years old) are drawing together on the iPad. They are playing the game Squiggle, which involves one of them starting a drawing and the other child finishing the drawing off. It is the turn of Child A to start the drawing. Child B is gazing intently at the iPad. They have a conversation about the drawing as it develops:

B: agaaahhhhh

A: ahh ahhh

B: that looks like a mouse, now it looks like a dinosaur

A: It's a dinosaur

B: I knew it's a dinosaur. I want one colour . . . arugh, what's this?

A: What's that?

B: Oh no, not dotty again

A: It's so funny

B: Weeee, that's better

A: It's like a squiggly . . . like a squiggly snake . . .

B: It looks like a slide that's so squiggly

A: It looks like a . . . wow, colourful

B: With lots of colours

A: That's the rainbow one

B: I love rainbows

A: Once I saw three rainbows

POSSIBILITY THINKING IN DIGITAL PLAY

Possibility thinking is a way of thinking about imagination and creativity. It marks the shift from thinking about 'what is' to 'what might be' or 'what if' (Cremin, Burnard & Craft, 2006; Craft, McConnon & Matthews, 2012). When we engage in possibility thinking, we change our thinking from what is actually in front of us to thinking about what might happen or what is possible with the resources that are around us. Possibility thinking is a fundamental aspect of children's play. In the explanations of play put forward by both Bruce (2012) and Sutton-Smith (2001), there is a focus on the way that play opens up the potential for things to become representations of another. For example, when a child pretends that a banana is a telephone as part of their role play, they are engaging in possibility thinking, since they have stopped thinking about the banana as a banana, and have engaged with the potential of the banana to represent another object and contribute to an unfolding drama as a result of this representation. Sutton-Smith describes how young humans, but also other species of mammals, engage in a kind of rough and tumble play that relies on some behaviours being taken as a playful representation of another behaviour, for example nipping becomes a representation of biting without involving the pain of biting.

The research of Craft and colleagues at the Open University around possibility thinking suggests that there are seven key characteristics of possibility thinking as it unfolds among children (e.g. Burnard et al., 2006; Chappell, Craft, Burnard & Cremin, 2008). These features are being imaginative, innovation, playfulness, risk-taking, self-determination, question-posing and immersion. Not all of these features are present in the same moment when possibility thinking is occurring, but all have a role to play in a sequence of possibility thinking. Playfulness might have more of a role to play in the early stages of possibility thinking when we are still exploring all the possible 'what ifs' with our resources and environment, while self-determination and immersion are more likely to develop later in the sequence of possibility thinking when a particular 'what if' solution has been committed to and is being developed in more depth.

How might possibility thinking manifest differently in the context of digital play? The journey of 'what if' thinking will be shaped by the particular affordances of the technologies involved in the digital play. If children are encouraged to engage in game-playing through digital technologies, where all of the rules in the game are prescribed, this could infringe upon the opportunities for possibility thinking since children are encouraged to engage with rules that have already been created by someone else, rather than making up their own rules. However, videogames do not always have to have clear rules. While we typically think about videogames as coming with embedded rules, alternative genres of videogames are developing that place less emphasis on rules and more emphasis on open-ended exploration. Trafi-Prats (2019) describes her daughter engaging in play through a computer game called Lumino City. Lumino City is a videogame characterised by the open-ended exploration of different places and landscapes, and machines placed in these worlds. Games like this are world-making games – the point is not to win according to predetermined rules, but instead to explore different contexts, and through both the imagination of the game designers and the imagination of the game players create a new, alternative world. These games seem to embody the spirit of possibility thinking in a way we do not typically associate with digital play.

Beyond gaming, digital play can offer resources that enable possibility thinking to flourish. In the conversation of the children drawing collaboratively together on the iPad, we see each of the seven features of possibility thinking:

- Playfulness: the children show playfulness through their spontaneous vocalisations and shared positive affect, smiling and giggling together.
- Risk-taking: the children engage in immediate touch, suggesting that they are not anxious about starting the task.
- Question-posing: although the children do not phrase their suggestions about what the line might represent as questions, none of the representations are taken to be conclusive but instead are treated as starting points for further suggestions. For example, when A says, 'it's a dinosaur', this does not preclude it from being something else, and they go on to brainstorm together lots of possible representations.
- Immersion: both children are intent on the activity; we can see this through the direction of attention towards the iPad at all points in the activity.
- Self-determination: there is purposefulness in the actions even though there is no clear endpoint; the exploration is purposeful – actions are swift, attention is focused and there is momentum in the engagement.
- Being imaginative: the potential representations that arise – the dinosaur, the rainbow, the slide – are all possibilities in the line that is generated through the iPad. The app on the iPad shifts colour spontaneously and this opens up further possibilities in terms of representation, suggesting that the creativity of the episode is a kind of dialogue between the children and the app they are using.
- Innovation: there are large jumps in the possibilities of representation, from a mouse to a dinosaur, to a squiggly snake, to a slide, to a rainbow and so on. None of the other children in this study went through the same sequence of ideas, suggesting scope for originality.

The theory of possibility thinking is helpful not just as a frame for thinking about children's creativity, but as a way in to thinking about how adults support children's imagination and creativity. Research by Cremin et al. (2006) suggests that there are three key pedagogic strategies that support children's possibility thinking, as follows:

1. Standing back – this involves adults taking a step away from children's activity, so that children feel that the locus of control is with them and that they have the freedom to develop the activity in the direction that they would like.
2. Profiling learner agency – this is when adults place emphasis on the child's choice and their ideas. Practically, this might look like an adult reflecting the question 'What should we do?' back towards the child, and stopping themselves from making a contribution

that would eclipse the child's own ideas. It also appears as a kind of permissiveness in activities, for example, as when children want to take activities in a direction that the facilitator hadn't anticipated, but the adult facilitator is willing to follow the children's lead and see where the activity goes next.

3   Giving time and space – this means adults simply making time available and constructing environments that are appropriate for possibility thinking. Children need 'stretchy time' (Cremin et al., 2006; Davies et al., 2013) to engage in possibility thinking, unrushed by adult-created deadlines. They are also supported by environments that offer both physical freedom – fluid movement through space, and the potential for combinations of resources to be used conjointly – and also environments that offer provocations to creativity and imagination, that is, fertile creative environments (Tarr, 2004; Strong-Wilson and Ellis, 2007).

In the activity described on p.67 we can see all of these pedagogic strategies in action. The researcher/teacher has taken a step away from the task, enabling the children to develop their ideas together. The children have the freedom to make their own choices and see where the activity goes next, and a key part of the time and the space is the iPad itself and the Kids Doodle app, which the children are engaging with. We can apply the same expectations that we have of physical environments, in relation to stimulating creativity and imagination, to digital environments. The Kids Doodle app appears to offer a balance between stimulation (e.g. the spontaneously changing colour of the line) and freedom (e.g. offering not much more than a line that changes in position, colour and tone).

Later research on pedagogic strategies to support possibility thinking has focused on the role of co-playing and the interest of adults in getting involved (Craft et al., 2012). The researchers described this as 'meddling in the middle', highlighting that sometimes rather than taking a step back, adults could take on the role of co-players and, through their genuine interest and enjoyment, facilitate children's possibility thinking. This manner of facilitation relies on adults feeling comfortable in the creative context, and when the activity is digital play this might not be as natural or instinctive. Previous research suggests that adults can be quite uncomfortable about getting involved in children's digital play and take a step back too much of the time, only coming to engage with children's digital play when things go wrong (Plowman & Stephen, 2005). This might be for practical material reasons, such as the difficulty of lots of people huddling around a screen together, but it might also be due to practitioners feeling uninspired or inexperienced in digital play contexts. There is therefore a need for practitioners to upskill themselves and get genuinely excited about the digital play possibilities, for example by finding games and applications that they themselves enjoy and would like to share with children.

RESEARCH SPOTLIGHT

Kucirkova, N., & Sakr, M. (2015). Child–father creative text-making at home with crayons, iPad collage & PC. *Thinking Skills and Creativity, 17,* 59–73.

AIMS

The aim of this study was to investigate how different resources – both digital and non-digital – would shape the possibility thinking of a 3-year-old child and her father as they engaged in art-making together. The researchers were interested to see whether the digital resources (art-making software on a laptop computer and iPad photography) would lead to different manifestations of possibility thinking from the non-digital resources (drawing with crayons on paper, collage using coloured card and stickers on paper). They were also interested in the father's involvement when these different resources were in use – would the pedagogic strategies used by the father to support the child's possibility thinking be different depending on the resources used? Would there be a digital/non-digital divide when it came to possibility thinking in the context of collaborative child–adult art-making?

METHODS

The researchers observed the child and her father making art together across eight episodes over a period of 3 months. In these eight episodes, the pair used four different sets of semiotic resources (two digital, two non-digital) for two episodes each. The child and the father engaged in these episodes of art-making in the home of the child's grandparents, which was a familiar and comfortable environment. The pair were video recorded by Sakr (who is also the child's aunt and therefore familiar to both participants). The videos were transcribed and the transcripts were annotated in relation to a) the seven different features of possibility thinking and b) the pedagogic strategies used by the father to support possibility thinking. Comparisons were made across the different semiotic resources to see how each set of resources impacted distinctly on possibility thinking and the collaborative nature of the task.

FINDINGS

The researchers traced how the different resources shaped possibility thinking in distinct ways, as a result of both their material properties and their social associations. For example, they noted that an important material property of both the collage activity and the art-making via the laptop was that the child and the father felt free to continue

(Continued)

editing the work through sticking/placing visual material on top of what was already on the page. This seemed to facilitate more risk-taking, while drawing via the crayons involved more apprehension on the part of the child, who was concerned about getting it 'wrong' and others responding negatively to what she had drawn. The findings did not suggest any clear distinction between digital and non-digital resources. Instead, each set of resources had particular affordances that shaped possibility thinking and the father's involvement, and these were more about the specific properties and associations of the resources, as opposed to whether the resources were digital or not. Thus, the findings support the view that possibility thinking is not necessarily hindered in digital play contexts, but that we need to be aware of the specific features of particular digital play contexts and how these might impact on creativity, child–adult interactions and collaborations more broadly.

REFLECTION ACTIVITIES

- Observe a child or children engaged in digital play. They might be playing a videogame or engaging in creative play, for example through an art-making app on a phone or tablet. If possible, video record the observation so that you can carry out the analysis in more detail. Focus your analysis around the seven key features of possibility thinking: playfulness, immersion, innovation, risk-taking, question-posing, being imaginative and self-determination. Watch the video (or a segment of the video) seven times, each time with a different characteristic in mind, making notes about whether you can see that feature in the behaviours of the child/children.

- Observe yourself with a child engaging in digital play. If possible, video record the observation. As you watch the video, make a note of the pedagogic strategies that you see yourself using in order to support possibility thinking (standing back, profiling learner agency, making time and space or meddling in the middle). How were the strategies you used shaped by the particular play context and the features of the digital technologies involved in the play?

- Find a digital play context that you are genuinely excited by. This might be an app that you find really fun or it might be an exploratory videogame like Lumino City. Find something that is appropriate to share with children and see what happens when you share something you're excited by. When you're co-playing, ready to meddle in the middle, how does the interaction unfold as a result? Write a reflection after the experience focusing on how this approach to setting up a digital play context shaped the way that possibility thinking and collaborative creativity manifested during the play episode.

CASE STUDY 5.2

STAMPS ON THE INTERACTIVE WHITEBOARD

Children are making art on the Interactive Whiteboard (IWB) during free-flow activity time in a reception classroom of 4–5-year-old children. Liam is on the board, with a few other children clustered around behind him, watching as he creates through the large IWB screen.

Liam starts his go. There are two fish already on the screen canvas, put there by the child previously having a go. Liam starts to put different shapes on top of the fish in different colours. To get a better look at what he has done, he steps down from the stool and comes over to the laptop – this is easier to view because the sunlight coming into the classroom from a window above creates glare on the big IWB screen.

Liam selects the image of a penguin from the 'stamps' collection inside Tux Paint, the art-making software installed on the IWB. He applies the penguin stamp over and over to the screen. This creates a repetitive noise, each time the image is applied – a repeated thudding that is quite oppressive but also quite hypnotic. He picks another colour and shape and lets his fingers wander – covering over the penguins.

Liam only stops his go when another child in the class comes over and asks him whether it can be her turn now. This seems to break Liam's concentration and he moves away from the board shortly after this interruption.

READY-MADE OR REMIX?

One key difference between digital and non-digital environments is the prevalence of ready-made material – whether the material is images, sounds or a pre-designed package of entertainment – rather than something that you have to imagine for yourself. In the observation above, the children are using the software *Tux Paint* in their creative play, which offers ready-made images through the 'stamp' tool. The images that are offered are lots of different types – from photographs of mundane objects (e.g. jugs, nutcrackers) to cartoon versions of fantastical creatures (e.g. ghosts, aliens). The stamps are grouped according to themes of content. The stamp tool comes as a particular multimodal package so that when you apply a stamp image, there is a particular sound that the software makes, and there is a predetermined written caption along the bottom of the screen that relates to the content of the image, for example a stamp of a penguin might have the written caption 'Penguin!' or 'Waddle along!'. This is different from using non-digital resources in creative play. Typically, making art through paper will not involve ready-made images, and if it does (e.g. as with collage, or using stickers), the images are not part of a predetermined multimodal package – there are no particular written captions or sounds that accompany the application of images.

In relation to non-digital environments, some researchers and practitioners have suggested that templates and ready-made adult materials are damaging to children's creativity and their own imaginative development. For example, McClennan (2010) and Szyba (1999) lament the use of adult-created visual materials in early years learning environments – whether this is colouring books or stencils or stickers. They suggest that children's own creativity is closed down by the provision of these materials, since rather than imagining things for themselves, they are relying on adult-made materials. Furthermore, they may have less confidence in the development of their own representations because they are comparing their own products to those of adults, so that, for example, a sticker of an alien might make a child think 'this is what an alien must look like' rather than engaging with the full and exciting range of possibilities involved in representing something fantastical like an alien. When we take this thinking into digital environments, we can see why there might be even more concern. Digital environments for creative play often involve the provision of lots of different types of ready-made materials. Does this limit the scope children have to imagine things for themselves?

However, even in the context of non-digital environments for creative play, there is a strong counter-argument that we need to consider. Before digital environments were part of the picture, a similar debate in childhood art education arose around the act of copying. Some researchers and practitioners argued that children should not be encouraged to make copies from other visual material, because this would inhibit their own imagination and visions for how to represent the world visually. However, Wilson and Wilson (1977; and later, Paul Duncum developed this line of inquiry to a great extent – see Duncum, 1999, 2010, 2019) argued that copying was in fact a starting point for creativity rather than something that hindered. They argue that there is actually no type of art-making that does not involve some kind of copying. From a sociocultural perspective, when we look at children's creativity, we see that it is always a response to what is in the world around the child – there is nothing that comes as a 'pure' expression of the child's inner world; in fact there is no such thing as the 'inner world'. All of what the child thinks and imagines is a re-working of what they experience in the world around them.

With the development of digital forms of creativity, this argument has been taken forward through the terms 'remix' and 'mash-up'. Lankshear and Knobel (2006) use the term 'digital remix' to describe the creative activities of children and young people via digital technologies. The term 'remix' highlights how children are using materials that already exist – these might be the ready-made images available in Tux Paint – and putting these together in their own unique imaginative and innovative way. Just as Wilson and Wilson (1977) argued about copying as a fertile basis for originality, so the theory of digital remix makes this the case in relation to ready-made digital materials. The materials will always need to be combined and applied in ways that constitute 'remix', and the act of remixing is itself creative. Lamb (2007) takes the idea of remix further in his conceptualisation of the 'mash-up', which is the use of digital data and/or systems in ways that were unintended or unanticipated by designers of the digital environments. This highlights the imagination and innovation that can be involved in working with ready-made materials that are already supplied in a digital environment, as well as suggesting the transgressive potentials of this, which is the focus of the next section of the chapter.

RESEARCH SPOTLIGHT

Björkvall, A. (2014). Practices of visual communication in a primary school classroom: Digital image collection as a potential semiotic mode. *Classroom Discourse*, 5(1), 22–37.

AIMS

This research study investigated how 7–8 year olds in a classroom context engaged in collecting digital images through the internet. The researcher was interested in how these digital images were part of the children's creative text-making and how the children thought about and organised the images as part of their meaning-making. Part of the study's aims were to consider how the children's collections of digital images related to other forms of collecting practice that they engaged in via non-digital environments, such as their collections of toys or football cards.

METHODS

The research was conducted through a social semiotic ethnography. This involved observation over a period of time with a focus on semiosis – that is, the meaning-making activities of participants in a community. Over just less than 2 years, the researcher made multiple visits to the same classroom of 7–8-year-old children. Gathering video data, fieldnotes, and text and image collections, the focus of the research was to see how children engaged with digital images, used these as part of creative text-making, and how the images related to the personal lives of the children and the life of the community in the classroom.

(Continued)

FINDINGS

The findings from the study demonstrate the various purposes to which the children's digital image collections related. Finding and organising images was often a highly social activity, with children connecting to one another around the images that they found and saved on their computers. The images also worked to connect the children's personal interests outside of the classroom (e.g. cars) with their engagement in the classroom context. The children in the study were also observed using the images in creative ways. For example, the images were used as part of multimodal slide show presentations that the children created as part of specific learning projects. The images were used to denote specific things (e.g. this is a rabbit), but also in order to connote general values and qualities more openly (e.g. using the image of a rabbit to connote cuteness). Björkvall's research suggests that even the acts of finding, selecting and saving pre-existing digital images can be understood as creative and as part of an active meaning-making process.

REFLECTION ACTIVITIES

- Work with the debate outlined above through observations in a non-digital environment. Ask children to engage in a copying activity, for example copying an illustration from a book or magazine. What creativity emerges through the copying activity? If you video record your observation, you could apply another analytical lens by considering the features of possibility thinking that you observe in this context.

- Engage in a digital remix activity with children. For example, you could create a video together that 'mashes up' existing ready-made sound clips, images, or moving images. A simple app like 'Our Story' will enable you to do this kind of activity even with very young children. Document how creativity manifests through the processes of remix in this digital play environment. What choices do children still have control over when they are working with ready-made materials?

CASE STUDY 5.3

ALEXA, DO YOU LIKE MONA?

We're in a den at the bottom of the garden. I'm interviewing my 4-year-old nephew, R, about his engagement with the personality of Alexa through the device the Amazon Echo. His family are keen users of Alexa – they have multiple devices scattered across the house, including one device in the den. I ask R to show me what sorts of things he asks Alexa.

> R turns to Alexa and asks 'Alexa, Alexa, do you like Mona?'
>
> Alexa replies 'I don't have an opinion on that'.
>
> R laughs loudly and starts pointing at me. He is grinning, clearly excited by the response. He bounces off the sofa in the den and says loudly 'that means she doesn't like you!'.
>
> 'Oh no' I reply, 'If she'd said, yes I'm always happy to meet new people, does that mean she does like me?'
>
> R replies, jabbing his finger in the air repeatedly 'That means, that means, that means she wants to marry them'.

TRANSGRESSIVE DIGITAL PLAY

R's engagement with Alexa above demonstrates how children can make use of the affordances (see Chapter 1 for an explanation of the term 'affordances') of different digital tools as a way of testing boundaries in social situations. This is a particularly imaginative use of digital technologies, and is often unanticipated by designers of technology. When it comes to natural user interfaces, such as The Echo, inhabited by the conversational agent (CA) Alexa, there is interesting research to show the ways that children use their imagination to experiment in their interactions with the technology in order to explore social etiquette and possibilities for social relationships. Druga, Williams, Breazeal and Resnick (2017) carried out observations of 26 children aged between 3 and 10 years old as they interacted with different CAs popular in the home, including Alexa, Google Home and Cozmo. The researchers observed children asking questions of the CA that would not be common among adults, including questions about the personality of the CA such as 'What is your favourite colour?', questions about the nature of the CA, such as 'What are you?' and 'Who made you?', and a few instances of children playfully testing boundaries, such as when a 6-year-old girl asked Alexa, 'Is it ok if I eat you?'.

We can think about this kind of engagement with digital technologies as transgressive play, in the sense that it transgresses the expected use and engagement that designers had in mind when the technology was originally developed. Marsh, Plowman, Yamada-Rice, Bishop and Scott (2016), whose article is the focus of the Research Spotlight below, suggest that transgressive play is a growing force in children's play when we focus particularly on digital contexts and forms of play. They suggest that we should enhance existing taxonomies of play – such as Hughes' (2002) popular playworker taxonomy of play, which identifies and explores 16 play types that are of significance in children's lives – to include transgressive play in digital environments. Marsh et al. (2016) were drawn repeatedly in their observational research in homes and classrooms to children's use of digital apps in ways that were unexpected, for example observing children as they made use of the music within gaming apps as part of their role play episodes, but not actually playing the game that the app was designed around. These types of play episode demonstrate that even though digital environments designed for children might seem to include lots of boundaries and rules, which we might see as in conflict with our conceptualisations of free-flow play, we need to pay attention to how children actually play in these digital environments, since they might often not adhere to the boundaries and rules.

In previous research looking at 4–5-year-old children's collective engagement with digital art-making on a computer laptop, it was fascinating to see the extent to which children thought up new and shared storylines to explain and develop their digital play, that went far beyond the prompts actually provided within the digital environments (Sakr, Connelly & Wild, 2016). The children in this study remade lots of the activities they engaged with on screen in new ways. For example, the activity of filling a screen with a new colour in Tux Paint – associated with the traditional symbol of the paint can tipping over – was re-made by the children as 'flooding'. Children talked about flooding the screen, shouting out 'oh no the flood is coming' when children applied a new colour to the screen. Over the course of the observations, the children developed this metaphor further, so that sometimes they talked about the 'jelly flood' and other times about the 'mud flood'. These ways of thinking and talking about the activity on screen show how children's own collective imagination and their creative dialogues with one another give another layer to the activity involved in digital play, which we must not ignore. In order to see the imagination involved in digital play, we need to look closely at how children's engagement actually unfolds, rather than limiting our analysis to just the nature of the digital environments targeted at children. While digital play environments might sometimes seem quite uninspiring, this will not necessarily mean that children's activities within these spheres will be unimaginative.

RESEARCH SPOTLIGHT

Marsh, J., Plowman, L., Yamada-Rice, D., Bishop, J., & Scott, F. (2016). Digital play: A new classification. *Early Years*, *36*(3), 242–253.

AIMS

The aims of this study were to explore play and creativity in children's engagement with different digital apps, and to consider what features of apps are effective in facilitating children's play and creativity. In this particular article, the researchers focus on applying an existing taxonomy of play – Bob Hughes' (2002) playworker taxonomy of play, which includes 16 play types. They were interested to see how the taxonomy related to observations of children's play involving digital apps – would the 16 play types be visible in this kind of digital play, and were there any additional types of play that are apparent in children's engagement with apps?

METHODS

The data explored in this article comes from a wider research study that involved a variety of methods, looking at the engagement of children aged 0–5 years with digital apps. The wider study involved a survey of parents, in-depth case studies of six children including video observations in their homes of them engaging with apps, analysis of app design, and observations of children using a variety of popular apps in a classroom context. This article considers the video observations that were collected as part of the research, both in homes and in a classroom context, and examines each observation of play in relation to Hughes' (2002) taxonomy of play.

FINDINGS

The researchers found that Hughes' taxonomy of play worked well in relation to the examples of children's engagement with digital apps. The researchers found all but two of the 16 play types described by Hughes in action in the context of the children's digital play. The two types of play that were not visible in children's engagement with apps were 1) rough and tumble play, which enables children to explore heightened physical contact, as well as aggression, in a safe environment, and 2) recapitulative play, which is play that connects us to our deepest human instincts, such as play involving the elements of fire and water, or storytelling in almost tribal settings. The researchers also found another type of play that they suggested was not represented in Hughes' taxonomy: transgressive play. Transgressive play involves children using apps in unexpected ways, that are unanticipated by the designers of the app. Identifying the play type of 'transgressive play' puts a focus on how children make use of the digital resources that are available to them in highly imaginative ways, and work in dialogue with designers, rather than simply responding to whatever digital designers make available to them.

REFLECTION ACTIVITIES

- Following the research of Marsh et al. (2016), conduct some of your own video observations of children engaged in playing with popular apps. Analyse these video observations in relation to Hughes' taxonomy of play. What types of play do you see in children's play with apps? Do you also find examples of transgressive play, as Marsh et al. found?

CHAPTER SUMMARY

- In this chapter, we have considered the theory of possibility thinking as a way of conceptualising imagination and creativity in relation to digital play environments. There are seven key features of possibility thinking (immersion, innovation, risk-taking, question-posing, playfulness, being imaginative, self-determination) and these can all be impacted in distinct ways by different digital environments. However, there is no research that suggests that any of these features of possibility thinking become impossible in the context of digital play, so we should remain open-minded about the opportunities for imagination and creativity in children's digital play.

- Pedagogic strategies to support possibility thinking (including standing back, profiling learner agency, creating time and space, and meddling in the middle) might be negatively impacted in relation to digital play as a result of adults' lack of confidence and experience with different digital environments.

- One of the key concerns around children's imagination and digital play is the prevalence of ready-made materials (e.g. images, sounds) in environments for digital play. However, there is a growing body of research that demonstrates how imagination and creativity are part of remixing ready-made materials. From a sociocultural perspective, all creativity involves drawing on what is already out there, so practices of 'remix' are central to imagination and creativity in non-digital environments as much as in digital environments.

- We need to be aware of the potential of children to imaginatively subvert the designers' expectations in their engagement with digital play environments. Research by Marsh et al. (2016) found that children often involved digital technologies in their play in ways that are unanticipated by the designers. They show imagination and playfulness that go beyond the properties and functionality of the digital environment, and so limiting our analysis to the technologies themselves is problematic and gives us an unfair view of the relationship between imagination and digital play.

RESEARCH ACTIVITIES

- Interview parents and practitioners about their views around digital play and imagination. A common opinion expressed in popular media is that digital play is damaging for children's imagination because digital environments are over-stimulating, and mean that children don't have to imagine things for themselves. Do the parents and practitioners you interview agree with this perception, or have they seen children in their classes or homes who have engaged imaginatively during episodes of digital play?

- By searching online, find out the top ten apps that are popular among young children at the time that you are reading this chapter. Download as many of these apps as you can. Analyse each app in relation to the question 'How does this app support a child to be imaginative?', highlighting which features of the app you feel will be helpful to children's imagination, and which features might hinder their imagination and creativity.
- Following on from the Research Activity above, conduct observations of children actually engaging with these apps. Does their play in these different app environments surprise you at all, or does it fit with your expectations when you analysed the apps prior to interaction? What examples of 'transgressive play' as described by Marsh et al. (2016) do you observe?

FURTHER READING

- Craft, A. (2012). Childhood in a digital age: Creative challenges for educational futures. *London Review of Education*, *10*(2), 173–190.

Anna Craft argues that as children and young people engage with new digital environments all the time, they are constantly acting as possibility thinkers, posing the question 'what if?' about these environments and the activities they carry out within them.

- Lamb, B. (2007). Dr. Mashup or, why educators should learn to stop worrying and love the remix. *Educause Review*, *42*(4), 13–14.

Lamb introduces the concept of 'mash-up', which involves remixing different types of digital material, but also reworking this material in ways that were unexpected by the designers or producers of the original content. Lamb argues that mash-up practices are deeply exciting from an educational point of view, and should be embraced by educators and policy-makers as creativity in action.

- Sakr, M., Connelly, V., & Wild, M. (2018). Imitative or iconoclastic? How young children use ready-made images in digital art. *International Journal of Art & Design Education*, *37*(1), 41–52.

In this paper, Sakr et al. describe research with young children, looking at their playful digital art-making and how ready-made images are used differently as part of children's distinct play agendas. The paper demonstrates the plurality involved in children's engagement with ready-made images, suggesting that our concern that digital ready-made materials make children less imaginative is unfounded.

6

DIGITAL PLAY AND MEDIA LITERACY

INTRODUCTION

In this chapter, we consider how children access new content through their digital play and the skills they and the adults around them require in order to make sense of what they encounter. This chapter:

- explores the competence and agency of children in using digital play experiences as a way of finding out more about the things they love and are interested in;
- examines how children's digital lives, particularly unboxing videos accessed through YouTube, mean that they can be targeted by companies as potential consumers without knowing that this is the case;
- considers the essential role of parents and carers in helping children to develop their media literacy, so that they access the information they care the most about in safe and critically engaged ways, enhancing their agency and autonomy as learners.

The chapter invites you to evaluate different media platforms and products in relation to these issues, as well as reflecting on the concerns and opinions of others, particularly parents and carers. The chapter is organised around observations of digital play and comments from parents, which are the starting point for discussing various relevant theoretical perspectives. In the Research

Spotlight sections you will find summaries of three pieces of recent research that look closely at children's digital play experiences and how aspects of information literacy play out as part of these experiences.

CASE STUDY 6.1

DISCO

Six young cousins (aged 18 months, 2 years, 33 months, 4 years, 5 years and 8 years old) are playing together as part of a family party. They go upstairs together to host a 'disco' in the bedroom of the 33 month old. The disco involves turning off the main light and putting on the lamp instead, which provides dimmer lighting. The oldest child, M, aged 8 years old, asks to borrow her dad's phone, which she takes upstairs. She accesses music through the Spotify app and selects songs for all the children to dance to. She is excited about selecting songs that are 'her favourite' and she often picks a new song before the previous song has come to an end. As they dance, the 4 year old references particular music videos that go with the songs. They show each other dance moves that they have picked up from videos. At one point, the 4 year old gets upset because he has 'run out of dance moves' and is worried that 'none of the dance moves are my own – they are all copied. I've copied them all. I just watch videos and copy them'. Adults in the family take it in turns to come up and check that the children are all safe and having a good time, but there is a clear distinction between the children and the adults in the family – the upstairs space has become the children's space while the adults engage in conversations downstairs. The children and adults are connected throughout this episode by the phone and the father's Spotify app which enables the children to have access to the music of their choice.

DIGITAL MEDIA AND KINDERCULTURE

The observation above demonstrates how children use digital play as a way to engage with the cultural products that are most relevant and enjoyable to them. They show impressive competencies when it comes to accessing music, videos or images that they are eager to engage with. Many other studies of children using digital technologies in the home highlight how children quickly learn to find the cultural products that they are most interested in and feel most relevant to their interests (Burnett et al., 2014; Marsh, 2017; Marsh, Hannon, Lewis & Ritchie, 2017; Squire & Steinkuehler, 2017; Burnett & Merchant, 2018). What children choose to engage with is often not the same as the digital technologies and media that their parents encourage them to use. Through their digital engagement, children construct their own subversive kinderculture (Thompson, 2003;

Kincheloe, 2011; Steinberg, 2011) – a culture shared between children that is markedly different from the cultural products that adults enjoy and recommend. In this particular observation, the children's music choices, and the rapid and frequent changes between different songs, as well as the dance moves that they have picked up from particular music videos, belong to a culture that they themselves have curated, though it has primarily been accessed through the digital technologies belonging to their parents and carers.

Kinderculture is not a digital phenomenon. The emergence of a culture and 'ket aesthetic' (Thompson, 2003) that is specifically enjoyed by children predates the development of digital media (Buckingham, 2007; Buckingham & de Block, 2007; Steinberg, 2011). For example, an important part of the children's activities in the observation above is how they share dance moves. Children sharing dance moves in the playground and showing each other the latest 'dance craze' is something that existed before the growth of the music video as an accessible cultural product for children (Bragg, Buckingham, Russell & Willett, 2011; Marsh & Bishop, 2012). However, even though kinderculture is not strictly a digital phenomenon, the emergence of digital media means that it manifests in new ways and becomes more widespread and easily accessible to children. As Craft (2013) notes, there are both advantages and disadvantages that emerge from this. On the one hand, we can take the ease with which children access the cultural products they most enjoy as an indicator of their growing agency and role as cultural producers and consumers. On the other hand, as children engage in kinderculture through a growing number of digital platforms, parents and carers understandably feel concerned that they have no way of protecting their children from what they perceive to be inappropriate cultural transactions (Livingstone, Mascheroni, Dreier, Chaudron & Lagae, 2015).

THE LATEST KINDERCULTURE CRAZE: 'BABY SHARK'

In Figure 6.1, children in an extended family are dancing to the music video for 'Baby shark'. You can see two of the children making the same moves that are shown in the video. You can also see one of the children more engrossed in their own digital tablet, and a younger child – 20 months old – watching intently the action both on the screen and among the children. This is a good visual example of children engaging in kinderculture through digital media. While we know what the two girls are engaging with, we cannot be sure what form of kinderculture the boy is engaging with through his tablet. What are your first impressions of this image? Which side of the debate does it appear to support – do the children strike you as agentive and capable, or do you feel fearful about their 'exposure' to kinderculture through different digital media? Perhaps you feel a mixed response, echoing the ambiguities noted by Craft (2013). Whatever your responses, note them down in order to see what different issues are arising and how these relate to the distinct theoretical perspectives highlighted above.

86 DIGITAL PLAY IN EARLY CHILDHOOD

Figure 6.1 Dancing to 'baby shark'

RESEARCH SPOTLIGHT

Pedersen, I., & Aspevig, K. (2018). Being Jacob: Young children, automedial subjectivity, and child social media influencers. *M/C Journal, 21*(2). Available at: http://www.journal.media-culture.org.au/index.php/mcjournal/article/view/1352

AIMS

Pedersen and Aspevig launched the project 'Kids, Creative Storyworlds and Wearables' to investigate what children make of their own digital futures. Through this ethnographic study, they developed a particular interest in the envisaged role of social media vlogging in children's future lives, and in this article, they deconstruct the vlogging of a particular child called 'Jacob'.

METHODS

The central project from which these data are drawn is an ethnographic study involving five children aged 4–7 years old. At the beginning of the project, the children were invited to reflect on what they thought the role of technology would be in their future lives. They were then given a smartwatch – the Kidizoom – through which they could make videos and photographs relating to these questions about their digital futures. The researchers were particularly interested in one 6-year-old boy in the study called Cayden, who was adamant that his future would involve setting up a successful online profile with the capacity to influence others through digital visual media. As a result of engaging with Cayden's responses, the researchers then focused on YouTube videos involving a boy 'Jacob' of a similar age. They consider Jacob's videos as an example of 'automedial subjectivity' – that is, indicative of how children might be constructing and presenting a 'self' through different digital media platforms now available to them.

FINDINGS

By framing Jacob as an 'automedial subject', and Cayden as a potential automedial subject of the future, the researchers highlight the role of digital visual media in children's lives and how this is intertwined with their developing sense of self and their relationships with others. They argue that Jacob is essentially selling his 'self' through social media. They offer concerns about his agency, but also suggest that he is likely to show increasing ownership around his vlogging as he gets older. Vlogging 'offers him a constrained, parent-sanctioned (albeit commercialised) space for role-playing, a practice bound up with identity formation in the life of most children' (p. 3). Thus, the vlogging is a way of making the self, but also more worryingly, a way of selling the self, before children are necessarily aware of exactly what they are offering up to the world and just how public these online environments are and will remain for their lives.

REFLECTION ACTIVITIES

- What recent examples have you seen of children engaging in the construction and consumption of kinderculture? What was the role of digital technologies within this? Were they using digital media as a way to access the cultural content that they wanted to engage with?

- Considering the Research Spotlight, what do you think about the idea of the 'automedial subject'? Watch some videos in which young children are sharing their 'selves' with others through YouTube. Type 'children vlog' into the YouTube search bar and you'll find some examples. What do you think about these practices? Are these children 'selling their selves' in a way that you find concerning? Or do you perhaps see them as creative and confident individuals who have the opportunity to express themselves in a way that children in the previous generation would not have had?

> ## CASE STUDY 6.2
>
> ### 'MY FAVOURITE TOY IS THE SUPER SOAKER'
>
> We are in the family 'den' at the bottom of the garden. 4-year-old R is showing me how he uses conversational agent Alexa (the virtual personality inhabiting Amazon's device 'The Echo') and the sorts of questions he asks Alexa. At one point in the conversation he asks 'Alexa do you like toys?'. Alexa replies 'Yes, in fact I love the super-soaker'. R looks to his father for an explanation because he does not know what a super-soaker is, and his father explains and mimes using one.

DIGITAL PLAY AND THE COMMERCIALISATION OF CHILDHOOD

In the observation above, we see an exchange that is designed to lead to a commercial transaction. Alexa's pronouncement that she likes the super-soaker could potentially, though it does not in this particular situation, lead to a child's follow-up questions – perhaps asking what a super-soaker is, or where they can find one of them and ultimately how to buy one. This highlights the 'grey area' that exists when it comes to the commercial targeting of children through new digital platforms and devices. What counts as advertising? Clearly, Alexa's response is not a traditional advertisement, but it does appear to be a prompt in the direction of a commercial transaction. Is a 4-year-old child likely to be aware in this kind of situation that they are being commercially targeted? Media literacy struggles to cover the bases of traditional advertising, to help children to disentangle the messages that they are sent about what they should want and how to buy it (or ask someone else to buy it), and yet in this instance, a child's media literacy needs to be even more extensive, to decode the commercial underpinnings of digital responses such as 'I love the super-soaker'.

Again, we return to Craft's (2013) reading of children's digital futures, in which she takes into account both sides of this equation. Children are potentially empowered and creative through their online experiences, but at the same time, we cannot romanticise their engagement with digital kinderculture. We need to remain aware of the political economy working 'behind the scenes' of their digital engagement and in particular how this involves the intensive targeting of children as commercialised objects of attention through myriad innovative means. Craig and Cunningham (2017) discuss these matters in relation to the YouTube phenomenon of 'unboxing'. In unboxing videos, children are filmed as they unwrap new toys and try out the toys for the first time.

As Craig and Cunningham note, the videos have been somewhat demonised in both popular and academic contexts, described as 'toddler crack' by Kollmeyer (2015), for example, because they are highly addictive and destructive, and Karageorgiadis (2016) suggests that both the children creating and those watching these unboxing videos are subjects of exploitation by the transnational corporations whose toys are being unboxed. On the other hand, Marsh (2016), as you will read in the Research Spotlight, presents a rather different picture, suggesting that the children watching do not necessarily want the toys that are unboxed in these videos. She highlights the vicarious pleasure of watching someone else unwrap something new, and that this might well trump the desire to have that item for oneself.

Unboxing videos on YouTube Kids, launched in 2015, have been the subject of official complaints filed by numerous media watchdog organisations concerned that children are targeted through such videos without knowing it. Despite this, unboxing videos remain remarkably popular and highlight the extreme need to constantly update children's media literacy. What does it mean to be media literate in contemporary society? Will this be the same in 10 years, or even 5 years? Martinez and Olsson (2018) explored children's media awareness in their discussions with 9–12-year-old children about the videos of a particular vlogging child – Misslisibell. Even though these children were in middle childhood, older than the 0–8 year olds we are particularly considering, only a few of them were aware of the relationship between Misslisibell's videos and advertising.

RESEARCH SPOTLIGHT

Marsh, J. (2016). 'Unboxing' videos: Co-construction of the child as cyberflâneur. *Discourse: Studies in the Cultural Politics of Education*, 37(3), 369–380.

AIMS

Marsh's research involved an investigation of the digital literacy practices of a young child across the home and school environments. Through this investigation, she focused particularly on a 4-year-old boy's experience and enjoyment of 'unboxing videos' on YouTube, in which he would watch another child opening boxes of toys. Marsh considered what this meant for his literacy practices, but also in relation to thinking about children as consumers and play as a transmedia phenomenon (i.e. something that crosses different media formats and platforms).

(Continued)

METHODS

The research revolves around a case study of a 4-year-old boy called Gareth, and Marsh's interest is in his literacy practices across home and school. She observed Gareth over the course of 4 months. In this time, there were 5 days in which she observed him over the course of the school day, and then on 4 of these days, she went home with him to see what sorts of activities he got up to at home after the end of the school day. The observations were written up through fieldnotes, and some photographs were included in the dataset. Marsh applied a thematic analysis to the data in order to see how Gareth's literacy practices moved across home/school and offline/online spaces.

FINDINGS

Marsh observed how Gareth's interest in LEGO crossed over offline and online spaces. As well as playing with LEGO in the physical environment, Gareth was drawn towards watching YouTube videos about LEGO or involving LEGO play. Following on from this, Gareth started to follow unboxing videos on YouTube and was observed by Marsh taking great pleasure in this activity. As a result of these observations, Marsh suggests that Gareth was a 'cyberflâneur' in relation to the unboxing videos, meaning that he was 'enjoying the sights but not necessarily purchasing goods'. This challenges the common understanding of unboxing videos as basically deceptive advertising – Marsh suggests that the vicarious pleasure, aesthetic dimensions and emotional responses involved in watching and engaging with unboxing videos are more complex than with traditional advertising formats.

REFLECTION ACTIVITIES

- Watch some toy-unboxing videos on YouTube. What do you think they represent? Why do you think so many children are drawn to these videos? What is the appeal? Do you have any concerns as you watch these videos, either about the children in the videos or about those children who repeatedly engage with these videos?

- Watch the videos with a child or group of children. How do they make sense of the videos? Keep the conversation open and non-judgemental and take notes on what they say. What awareness do they show (if any) around the commercial dimensions of this kind of video? Do they show any desire to buy those toys for themselves, or as Marsh suggests, are they more interested in taking vicarious pleasure through watching the unboxing by another child?

> ## CASE STUDY 6.3
>
> ### WHAT PARENTS SAY ABOUT MEDIATION
>
> The following comments from parents about their children's engagement with digital media and what they are doing to mediate this relationship come from an ongoing research study conducted by Jacqueline Harding to understand more about the concerns of parents and what further support they require.
>
> > 'They are watching less TV (2 year old and 5 year old) – all have iPads – so I have to keep an eye on them. I'm always in the same room. I like to be with them so I can see.'
> >
> > 'My younger child (2 year old) finds and uses Peppa Pig on YouTube. They are so clever. So quick too.'
> >
> > 'It's different now – it's user driven not schedule driven – my child will use Netflix and YouTube. It's constant watching everything for safety.'
> >
> > 'I'm constantly asking her if she is OK and I look at what she is playing on the iPad.'
> >
> > 'My little one (15 months) is very interested in repetitive TV/video/YouTube – watches Buzz Lightyear over and over again . . . and I am aware of it – think he needs it so I don't turn it off.'
> >
> > 'I say "no" to the phone in the bedroom for my 6 year old.'
> >
> > 'I'm always asking if she is OK and I look at what she is doing.'

PARENTAL MEDIATION AND MEDIA LITERACY

Research suggests that parental mediation is essential in helping to develop children's awareness in their online activities, which in turn keeps them safe but also heightens their capacity to assess and potentially reject the commercial messages that they will encounter. In research by Duerager and Livingstone (2012) the parents of 142 9–16 year olds across 25 European countries were surveyed about their mediation of their children's online activities. They found that parents putting limitations in place around their children's online activities (e.g. when they can access the internet) did keep children safer in their online activities, but it also limited the opportunities for the development of knowledge, skills and shared positive affect in the family home. Technical mediation, such as the use of parental blocks and firewalls, were found to be ineffective in minimising risk. On the other hand, active mediation, underpinned by parents wanting to understand more about their children's online activities and engaging from a place of enjoyment, seemed to both minimise risk for the children and also heighten the opportunities for learning and shared positive experiences in the family. Similarly, Hefner, Knop, Schmitt and Vorderer (2019) surveyed 500 children aged between 8 and 14 years old and one of each child's parents, and found that open child–parent communication and positive relationships were essential in supporting children to use a mobile phone in a way considered by the researchers to be safe and supportive. Open, active communication between children and parents seems to be more effective than putting restrictions in place when it comes to helping children to navigate different digital environments, staying safe and being critically aware of the content they might come across.

Co-use among children and parents seems to be a particularly promising way for families to develop positive relationships around digital technologies and enable children to develop medial literacy skills. Beyens and Beullens (2017) found in a survey of 346 parents with children aged between 2 and 10 years old that while restrictive mediation was associated with child–parent conflict, co-use seemed to protect against unnecessary conflict. Building on Nathanson's (2002) arguments, the researchers argue that co-use facilitates bonding and can thereby reduce conflict that surrounds media use in the family home. Restrictive mediation (i.e. putting limitations about use in place) may be practically easier and less time-consuming, but not as impactful as finding the time to engage with what children are doing and finding shared passions that occur online. In research by Trafi-Prats (2019), she describes the pleasure that a daughter aged 7 years and father find in playing the alternative, non-competitive computer game 'Lumino City'. In this scenario, the father is not indulging the child through his co-use, but is doing something which they both genuinely enjoy. This sets the basis for interesting and impactful conversations regarding lots of things, including the digital content that the child begins to access through the online spaces and the videogames:

Imagine . . . an interactive, or educative approach that engages parents in a dialogue about the quality of our interaction with media, encourage parents to nurture and build connections with children (and one another) through media, and promote *generative* media practices. (Squire & Steinkuehler, 2017: 12)

RESEARCH SPOTLIGHT

Squire, K., & Steinkuehler, C. (2017). The problem with screen time. *Teachers College Record*, 119(12), 1–24.

AIMS

The researchers problematise the notion of 'screen time' – the idea that there is a 'right' or 'healthy' amount of time that children can spend engaging with digital media. Instead, they seek to engage with the more complex dynamics at work in an ecosystem of play, as play moves between different types of media. They ask what other more interesting and important issues a preoccupation with limiting 'screen time' distracts us from, and what new opportunities for the lives of children and families open up when we prioritise monitoring quality over quantity.

METHODS

The researchers report on a case study of a single child, a 7 year old who they call 'Walt', living in the US. They conducted observations over a 3.5 month period, as well as numerous informal interviews over this time, revolving around Walt's interest in the American football videogame 'Madden' and how this is intertwined with myriad other activities in Walt's life. How does Walt make meaning around his playing of 'Madden' and how does it feature in his wider semiotic and social networks?

FINDINGS

The researchers find that the videogame 'Madden' scaffolds his understanding of American football more broadly. For example, the ratings of teams offered within the videogame and updated each season help him to understand the strengths and weaknesses of actual football teams. His episodes of videogame-playing always involve or are intertwined with other forms of play – for example physical play involving an actual football. Through their observations, the researchers document a complex ecosystem of play that involves the videogame Madden, physical football, football gossip, iPad football games, football cards, televised games of football, documentaries about football, playing football with peers in school, reading about football and writing stories about football. The researchers conclude that this ecosystem is indicative of how we (both children and adults) construct 'coherent (albeit transmedia) systems of meaning' (p. 11) that have no neat relation to offline/online dichotomies, moving continuously between different media and environments. 'Football' is Walt's hobby – rather than anything so specific as 'playing Madden' or 'watching football on television'; when we focus on the notion of 'screen time', we lose this connection to lived experience and we risk cutting children off when they are in the flow of pursuing particular knowledge, skills and passions.

REFLECTION ACTIVITIES

- Do you agree with Squire and Steinkuehler that 'screen time' is an unhelpful concept when it comes to thinking about children's digital lives. Map out the arguments for and against giving parents guidance around how much screen time to allow.

- Interview a parent about how they mediate their children's digital activities. Analyse their responses – are most of their actions based around restrictive mediation, technical mediation, active mediation or co-use? What advice would you give them on the research outlined in the previous section about how they could advance their mediation practices further and support their children not only to stay safe but develop essential digital and media literacy skills to enhance their future lives?

CHAPTER SUMMARY

- Children use digital technologies and online platforms to consume and construct their own 'kinderculture', that is, a culture that is markedly different from that enjoyed and encouraged by the adults in their lives.

- Kinderculture is not a digital phenomenon since it precedes children engaging with digital environments. However, digitisation means that kinderculture manifests in new ways and parents/carers may feel disconcerted by the pervasiveness of kinderculture as a result of children's digital connectedness.

- Digital kinderculture is characterised by new forms of commercialisation. There are particular concerns around children's exposure to commercial objectives that are not immediately apparent as a result of the format in which they appear, such as product placement in the responses of a digital conversational agent (e.g. Alexa) or popular unboxing videos on YouTube.

- Parental mediation is essential in helping children to stay safe online and become more critically aware of the different agendas that resonate through online environments, including commercial agendas.

- Research suggests that active mediation and co-use are more effective than restrictive or technical mediation in minimising the risk involved in children's online activities, and also in developing their opportunities to increase knowledge, skills and critical engagement. Co-use in particular leads to important exchanges between children and parents that become a strong foundation for media literacy in very young children.

RESEARCH ACTIVITIES

- Conduct a case study, focusing on one child between the ages of 3–8 years, investigating and mapping their personal interests and activities. Focus on one particular interest that they have, such as a particular character or storyline (e.g. Peppa Pig, *Frozen*), or an activity they are fascinated by (e.g. building blocks, dressing up dolls, pretend play of a particular type, LEGO or keeping pets). Just as Squire and Stienkuehler (2017) did in their research, map how this interest plays out for the child between online and offline spaces. How does the child's interest and passion move between these different environments? To support your analysis, map the activities in a visual way, so that you show how digital and non-digital activities are connected as children engage with their everyday interests.

- Inspired by the research of Martinez and Olsson (2018), conduct a focus group with young children analysing a particular vlog that is popular with under-8s.

Martinez and Olsson conducted a focus group with 9–12 year olds about their experience of a video from popular child vlogger Misslisibell. They asked the children open questions about what they took from the video and how they perceived it. Do something similar with the younger children in your focus group. How do they make sense of this video material? What are their impressions of it? What awareness do they show, if any, of the particular agendas that might be at work in a video like this?

- Conduct your own observation study of parental mediation in a particular household you have access to. Most studies of parental mediation have relied on surveys and interviews with parents. The problem with collecting data from parents in this way is that they can only report on what they remember and are conscious of, and also they may be inhibited in their responses because they want to be seen as 'getting it right' as a parent. Observation studies can be one way of gaining new insights into how parents actually mediate their children's digital engagement as part of their everyday life. You will need to recruit a family that feels comfortable with you – perhaps close friends or extended family members. Spend the day with them and observe parental mediation of the children's digital engagement as it unfolds. What do you see? Restrictive mediation? Technical mediation? Active mediation? Co-use? What conversations between children and parents are going on about the children's online activities?

FURTHER READING

- Craft, A. (2013). Childhood, possibility thinking and wise, humanising educational futures. *International Journal of Educational Research, 61*, 126–134.

Craft argues that we need to be careful not to fall into the trap of creating a false dichotomy between positioning digital technologies as either enhancing children's creative cultural production or as tempting children into a state of hyper-consumerism. She suggests that in our analyses of children's digital futures, we need to make room for both of these dimensions to co-exist. We need to see the opportunities for children to engage in creative digital practices that give them more control and choice in constructing and consuming kinderculture, while also remaining acutely aware of the different agendas that unfold in online environments, including the commercial agendas of powerful corporations with a significant online presence.

- Gillen, J., & Kucirkova, N. (2018). Percolating spaces: Creative ways of using digital technologies to connect young children's school and home lives. *British Journal of Educational Technology, 49*(5), 834–846.

Gillen and Kucirkova suggest ways of connecting home and school environments for young children through digital technologies. They suggest that digital links between home and school can help to develop digital literacy and learning practices in both of these environments, and create a stronger sense of flow between the environments. Through this home–school digital flow, adults in both settings have a chance to engage children in interesting conversations about their online activities and develop their media literacy.

- Martínez, C., & Olsson, T. (2018). Making sense of YouTubers: How Swedish children construct and negotiate the YouTuber Misslisibell as a girl celebrity. *Journal of Children and Media, 13*(1), 1–17.

Martínez and Olsson report on group interviews with 9–12 year olds following co-watching of a video posted by YouTuber Misslisibell. The researchers analyse the children's responses to the videos, looking at how the children make sense of celebrity in the YouTube environment and what they see as the purpose of such videos.

7

MANAGING ATTENTION IN DIGITAL ENVIRONMENTS

INTRODUCTION

In this chapter, we explore the relationship between attention and digital play environments. There is much popular concern about potentially negative impacts on attention as a result of frequent digital engagement. This chapter:

- presents research suggesting that there are particular 'cognitive shifts' as a result of increasing digital engagement in our lives, including more scattered attention. We consider whether these shifts, if they are the case, are necessarily 'maladaptive' or whether they might be occurring because they are best suited to the world we live in;
- examines the argument that increased digital engagement among children is causally linked to the rise of diagnoses of attention deficit and hyperactivity disorder (ADHD);
- considers whether fast-paced environments are an inevitable part of digital play, or whether alternative games can lead to slower forms of exploration and adventure, which in turn might allay our fears that attention is negatively affected by the rise of digital play.

As you will see, the chapter relies heavily on psychological research that has been conducted with adolescents and adults to look at how attention is distributed in digital environments. We should be aware that this research is problematic for our purposes for two reasons. Firstly, research on adults and adolescents is a poor indicator of what is happening among a much younger population. It has been necessary to draw on this research with older participants because of the lack of research that looks empirically at children's attention in digital environments. Secondly, psychological research typically depends on experimental settings that are constructed in laboratory conditions and do not always relate well to the sorts of experiences we have in our everyday lives. In order to counter these issues with the research that appears both in the theory sections and the 'Research Spotlights', the narrative observations and Reflection Activities throughout the chapter are designed to make connections from this research landscape to the everyday play experiences of young children.

CASE STUDY 7.1

A 1 YEAR OLD CONCENTRATING ON 'ANGRY BIRDS'

A 1-year-old child is playing the game 'angry birds' on their parent's tablet. They are sat on the dining room table, with the tablet resting on their lap. Their gaze is down at the screen on their lap. They are rocking slightly backwards and forwards. They tap the screen with urgency a couple of times and the visual display immediately changes. They bounce up and down in response with excitement. Their gaze flits around the screen, and only briefly leaves the screen – to look up with a smile at the person behind the camera. They tap the screen again, and when there is no response they briefly bash the screen with their whole fist. The visual display changes. They swipe the screen with their right hand and then with their left hand. They continue to look down with concentration. They have grown very still now and are no longer rocking or bouncing.

ALLOCATING ATTENTION IN DIGITAL PLAY ENVIRONMENTS

Some psychologists argue that cognitive processing is currently changing as a result of our engagement with digital environments and how attention is allocated in digital environments. For example, Loh and Kanai (2016) suggest several cognitive changes as a result of regular engagement with the internet. These include:

- shallower information processing, so that information is skimmed for what is relevant rather than engaged with more deeply;
- rapid attention shifting between different sources of stimulation rather than engaging with one thing at a time;

- less deliberation over information, so that information is either taken on board or rejected, but not considered or explored as thoroughly as before;
- more distractibility, so that we are more likely to be in a state where we are prepared to be stimulated by something else, whether it's a message that appears on our phone, or a notification from an app we frequently use; and
- poorer executive control, which is a consequence of the scattered attention, meaning that we have fewer attentional resources to allocate to resisting temptations of distraction.

As evidence of shallower information processing, Carr (2011) investigated participants' responses to hyperlinked texts. They found a correlation between the number of hyperlinks in a text and the shallowness of the information processing. They suggested that this was because each hyperlink required a greater allocation of cognitive resources; as a result, when there were more hyperlinks encountered by the reader, there were fewer cognitive resources to support in-depth thinking about the information encountered. In support of the view that we are less likely to take information on board in a deep or deliberate way when we engage with it in digital environments, Henkel (2014) found that photographing objects rather than just looking at them led to poorer recall of the properties of each object. This suggests that when we engage in digital activities that are about the storage of information externally, we can rely on these external stores of information. Fisher, Goddu and Keil (2015) refer to this as 'external transactive memory' – something external to ourselves that successfully stores information so that we do not have to. This is not necessarily a digital phenomenon (e.g. a list or a calculator has the same effect of distributing our cognitive resources), but psychologists such as Loh and Kanai argue that these practices and shifts in cognitive style are heightened as a result of the rise of digital mediation.

We need to remain aware that many of the studies conducted in this area have been completed with adult participants rather than children, and therefore relate to the digital activities that might be typical for adults but not for children (e.g. reading hyperlinked texts). More fundamentally, we need to consider whether these cognitive shifts – if they are indeed occurring – are not necessarily maladaptive. This means that we need to question whether such changes are necessarily bad in relation to the changing context in which we live. As Loh and Kanai themselves note, cognitive shifts are an inevitable consequence of technological development – and this is the case regardless of whether the technology is digital or not. The technology of writing developed thousands of years ago also seemed to lead to shifts in our cognitive processing, but this is not something that retrospectively we consider to be bad or unhelpful. Our minds work in line with the sociocultural context, and defining what is a 'good' or 'bad' adaptation in how the mind processes information and allocates attention depends on the cultural context. For example, Carrier, Rosen, Cheever and Lim (2015) show that multi-tasking behaviours are correlated with poorer academic performance, but perhaps this says more about our academic environments and what is expected within these environments, than about the maladaptation of human cognition. As demonstrated in the research by Mavoa, Gibbs and Carter (2017) on the discourse that surrounds digital technologies in education, particularly among practitioners, the tendency is to focus on 'loss' as a result of the rise of digital technologies, regardless of what the evidence shows. Thus, we might feel that we are 'losing' concentration as a result of digital environments, when actually our cognition is simply allocating attention in the most efficient way it can in that context.

SCATTERED ATTENTION IN A FAMILY ENVIRONMENT

In Figure 7.1, you can see two siblings – a 4 year old and an 8 year old – both engaged in digital play at the same time. Rather than engaging in the same digital play activity together, they are engrossed in their own digital devices. What you cannot see in the photograph is that the television is also on in the background. So there are three different digital devices being used in close proximity to the children – a smartphone, a tablet and a large television. The photograph shows some of the issues mentioned in the section above in action. In particular, a photograph like this might lead us to ask questions about attention-shifting practices around digital play and the distractibility of environments where there are a lot of digital stimuli on offer. What are your impressions of this photograph? Do you see the children's concentration or the potential for distraction? The photograph also relates closely to the Research Spotlight immediately following it, which discusses the impact of media multi-tasking (engaging with different digital devices simultaneously) on the distribution of attention.

Figure 7.1 Children engaging with different digital devices simultaneously

RESEARCH SPOTLIGHT

Brasel, S.A., & Gips, J. (2011). Media multitasking behavior: Concurrent television and computer usage. *Cyberpsychology, Behavior, and Social Networking, 14*(9), 527–534.

AIMS

This research study was conducted in order to find out more about how individuals navigate media multi-tasking situations, such as using a computer while at the same time watching a television. The researchers thought that this was important to investigate since previous survey research suggests that the majority of television-watching is now accompanied by browsing the internet on other devices. The researchers were interested in how individuals engage in multi-tasking, as compared with their perceptions of their own behaviours. Although this study focuses on the behaviours of adults, the results have implications for our understanding of how children engage with complex media environments and how their cognition and attention shifts as a result.

METHODS

The study was based around a laboratory experiment in which participants engaged with both a computer and a television over a 30-minute period as they were video recorded. There were a total of 42 participants in the study, equally divided into two age groups: 18–22 year olds, and 28–65 year olds. Video records of the participants as they engaged in the media multi-tasking environment were analysed in terms of where their gaze was at each second of the activity, and what this suggested about the switches in their attention between the television and the computer. The participants also completed a post-experiment survey, which included questions about their estimated level of switching between the television and computer, so that the researchers could see whether the participants had an accurate perception of their own multi-tasking behaviours.

FINDINGS

Analysis of the video observations showed that participants attended primarily to the computer as compared with the television, with longer gazes directed at the computer than the television. However, participants' behaviours overall were characterised by very short gazes, just a few seconds long, suggesting that there was a high frequency of switching between the different types of media available. On average, the participants switched their gaze four times per minute, and there was more switching in the younger group of participants when compared with the older group of participants. The results from the post-experiment survey showed that participants underestimated their switching behaviour, thinking that they had switched attention just 12% of what their behaviours actually showed.

REFLECTION ACTIVITIES

- Compare yourself with your parents (or someone you know in the generation of your parents). Do you notice differences between you in terms of how you divide attention and process information? Do the cognitive shifts suggested by Loh and Kanai (2016) work in relation to your own example? For instance, do you tend to process information more shallowly, and are you more distractible when engaging in a task?

- Create a diary of your media multi-tasking behaviours. Document each time you engage with digital technologies and media – how many devices are you using at the same time? Within the device, how many things are you attempting to complete or engage with at once?

CASE STUDY 7.2

'CHILDREN MIGHT FIND IT BORING': PRACTITIONER PERCEPTIONS ABOUT THE LEVEL AND TYPE OF STIMULATION REQUIRED BY CHILDREN WHEN THEY ENGAGE IN DIGITAL PLAY

In a workshop for practitioners exploring different apps available for young children aged 0–8 years, we investigated and reviewed the app 'Toca Nature'. Toca Nature is characterised by open-ended exploration of natural habitats, which are represented on screen through creative and calming visual displays. There is no clear goal or instructions for the app – children are free to explore the environments in their own way and at their own pace. The 20 early years practitioners attending the workshop were intrigued by the app, interested in the 'discovery/exploratory aspect' as well as the 'subtle investigation of conservation'. However, there were also concerns that children would lose interest in this kind of digital play environment – that without the clear goals, levels and fast pace of a typical digital play environment, children would lose patience and find it too boring. Despite these concerns, Toca Nature is a popular app among families. It is rated with four stars on the Common Sense Media website, and on Amazon, the reviews from parents suggest that children can find it compelling to create in careful and considered ways with the app, not necessarily needing the fast pace that the practitioners in the workshop assumed they would. For example, one Amazon review describes the following:

> Both me & my son (just turned 4) really adore this app. Simple but addictive, build a new landscape every time, harvest food, learn what foods each animal likes to eat to grow & feed the animals. It is a well made & very cute app, I recommend it.

FAST-PACED DIGITAL PLAY AND ATTENTION DEFICIT DISORDER: IS THERE A LINK?

In the section above, we suggested that whether we see shifts in cognitive style as maladaptive or adaptive depends on our cultural context. In an educational trajectory that values the ability to focus, the constant and rapid division of attention between multiple sources of attention may well be maladaptive. Kirschner and De Bruyckere (2017) argue that the term 'multi-tasking', which is often applied to digital engagement behaviours among both children and adults, is a misnomer. They argue that there is no such thing as 'multi-tasking' and that neuroscientific evidence actually shows that the brain is never carrying out two tasks simultaneously, but is instead conducting rapid shifts in attention between the two or more tasks that the participant is currently attempting to carry out. Salvucci and Taatgen (2008) refer to this as 'threaded cognition', and it is important to be aware of how this can be detrimental to completing learning tasks to a high standard. Every time we switch our attention between tasks, the mind requires some time to re-acclimatise to that other task, meaning that task-switching actually leads to inefficient completion of tasks.

In her book *Mind Change* (2014), Susan Greenfield makes the argument that the rise of digital technologies, including social media and videogaming, is responsible for significant negative neurological changes in individuals. These changes in the brain's structure underpin psychopathological disorders, such as attention deficit and hyperactivity disorders. In a response to Vaughan Bell, who accused her of scaremongering, she highlights the research showing that high levels of multi-tasking are associated with differences in brain structure and diagnoses of ADHD. Of course, correlation is not the same as causation. It might be that digital play and engagement has risen, and so have diagnoses of ADHD, but these contemporaneous rises do not necessarily mean that one has caused the other. Greenfield (2015) actually argues that the relationship works both ways – that individuals with attention problems are more likely to be drawn to the fast-paced digital play environments offered by videogames, and that videogame-playing – with its intensive stimulation and required task-switching – will lead to the scattered and inefficient allocation of attention – what Hayles (2007) describes as 'hyper attention'.

When considering Greenfield's arguments we need to remain aware – at the very least – of the age differences that relate to what children, adolescents and adults do when they engage with different digital technologies. The types of social media and videogaming that have been the focus of most of Greenfield's primary and secondary research are not actually applicable to most young children's experience (Selwyn, 2009). So even though ADHD as a diagnostic label is applied more frequently to even the youngest children, we need to consider the specific forms of digital play that may (or may not) be linked with this issue. And again, just as Mavoa et al. (2017) suggest, there is the need to zoom out and consider context in relation to these issues. For example, Ken Robinson (2010) makes the argument that ADHD as diagnostic label needs to be critiqued. It may be the medicalisation of what is actually a sociocultural issue – the irrelevance of educational content and styles of learning and teaching in contemporary educational settings. He argues that it is schools that need to adapt rather than individuals' behaviours.

RESEARCH SPOTLIGHT

Ra, C.K., Cho, J., Stone, M.D., De La Cerda, J., Goldenson, N.I., Moroney, E., Tung, I., Lee, S.S., & Leventhal, A.M. (2018). Association of digital media use with subsequent symptoms of attention-deficit/hyperactivity disorder among adolescents. *JAMA, 320*(3), 255–263.

AIMS

These researchers were interested to see whether there was a statistical correlation between the frequency of digital media engagement among adolescents and later manifestation of symptoms of attention deficit and hyperactivity disorder. They suggested that it was important to determine whether such an association existed because of the highly stimulating nature of contemporary digital environments used by children and young people. Although this study is with children older (adolescents) than those at the centre of our particular interest in this book, the research questions and findings are of interest in thinking about the experiences of younger children also.

METHODS

The researchers surveyed 3051 adolescents aged 15–16 year olds about the frequency with which they engaged with 14 different types of digital activity. They conducted follow-up surveys with the sample on four separate occasions – 6, 12, 18 and 24 months after the initial survey. In these follow-up surveys, the participants self-rated their own behaviours in relation to 18 symptoms associated with ADHD. The researchers carried out a statistical analysis to determine whether there was a statistically significant correlation between digital media use reported in the first survey and self-report of ADHD symptoms in any of the later surveys.

FINDINGS

Statistical analysis showed that high frequency use of each of the 14 digital activities asked about in the first survey was associated with a higher likelihood of self-reporting ADHD symptoms in the follow-up surveys. This association was modest but significant. The researchers highlight that the statistical correlation cannot tell us about causation – it does not mean that higher levels of digital engagement cause symptoms of ADHD to emerge and develop. It might be that there are other factors that are leading to a rise in both types of behaviour; for example, aspects of the home environment in which these children live may lead to both higher levels of digital engagement and manifestation of symptoms associated with ADHD. Further research is required in order to see whether there is a causal relationship.

REFLECTION ACTIVITIES

- How convincing do you find the link between digital technologies and ADHD? Map the evidence for and against the theory that there is a causal link, meaning that the rise in digital engagement is to blame for the rise in ADHD.

- Watch Ken Robinson's (2010) TED talk offering an alternative perspective on the nature of ADHD, what is to blame and what needs to change. Which argument do you find more convincing – Greenfield or Robinson? Is there a way to reconcile these different points of view?

CASE STUDY 7.3

LUMINO CITY

Lumino City is described by its makers as a 'handmade puzzle adventure' game. Lumino City has a particular aesthetic since the set for the game was made entirely out of paper, card, miniature lights and motors. The makers explain that it took 3 years to make the game – thus, the care and attention to detail is a key aspect of this game. Lumino City starts with a conversation between Lumi and her grandad. Her grandad has something he wants to explain to Lumi but he needs a cup of tea first. When Lumi goes to make her grandad a cup of tea, he is kidnapped, leaving behind only a book – a 'handy manual' which offers insights into how different things are made. Lumi heads out to the city to investigate and see whether she can find her grandad. As she goes she picks up items and stores them in a bag, solving puzzles that include how to get from one place to the next, how to unlock doors and even how to make electricity. The experience of playing Lumino City is shaped by the relaxed instrumental music in the background and the unusual and careful handmade aesthetics – these design features have the effect of slowing down the player. Although there are puzzles to be solved, they are all based around possibility thinking – question-posing and trying things out, using imagination to work out how to make the next move – and this is done at a pace that suits the user. There are no timers or countdowns, nobody is chasing you through the city – the pace belongs to the player.

SLOWING DOWN DIGITAL PLAY: WHAT THE INDEPENDENT GAMES INDUSTRY OFFERS

In explorations of creativity and imagination, researchers highlight the need for immersive experiences that involve sensory exploration that is slow and careful. For example, Denmead and Hickman (2012) conducted an interview study with adult artists about the materials that are part of their art-making process, and the affordances of these different resources. The artists held in common regard the importance of 'slowliness' – a term offered by Denmead and Hickman to refer to an 'immersive pleasure-state' involving careful, highly sensory exploration of different materials, where instead of focusing on what should be done with the materials, there is an appreciation of the materials themselves and the many possibilities at work within them. The artists interviewed in this study were generally sceptical about the potential of digital technologies to be associated with 'slowliness'. They suggested that most often digital environments encourage fast-paced involvement, where the emphasis is on rapidly finishing tasks, rather than engaging in a slowed-down way with the world around us. This relates to the views of early years practitioners reported in Sakr (2017), who felt that digital technologies were just 'not that early years-ish' because they did not encourage heightened sensory engagement.

However, trends in digital games design do highlight alternative possibilities for pace in digital environments. Newer digital play environments suggest that fast-paced playing is not the only possibility. Wilson (2005) surveys the independent games industry and shows how low-cost, independent game design and production bring both constraints and opportunities. One of the opportunities associated with independent games creation is the potential role of 'art-house values and modes of production' (p. 110), and these may in turn have the effect of 'slowing down' digital play. For example, one of the genres included in his survey is 'digital craft', which involves videogaming that actually comprises making your way through static scenes, solving puzzles and finding clues (like Lumino City in the observation). This 'highly engaging ludic practice' (p. 118) is completely slowed down, showing how digital games need not appear in a particular way in order to appeal to players. Similarly Lastowka (2012) discusses the appeal of Minecraft and other 'sandbox' games, where players are absorbed by creative making activity, rather than trying to 'win' a game in a particular way. Thibault (2016) describes games like Minecraft and Lumino City as 'post-digital games' and suggests that the constraints that they involve, the fact that the graphics are not photo-realistic and actually feel quite 'basic', can lead us to explore more creative possibilities in our actions as players. Slowed-down graphics 'can consistently represent dreamy situations' and 'can support artistic and emotional storytelling' (p. 11).

RESEARCH SPOTLIGHT

Wilson, D. (2011). Brutally unfair tactics totally ok now: On self-effacing games and unachievements. *Game Studies, 11*(1). Available at: http://gamestudies.org/1101/articles/Wilson

AIMS

In this study, Wilson explores alternative possibilities in game design, looking closely at the phenomenon of 'broken' games, which are computer games that require players to make up many of the parameters of the game for themselves, to negotiate and enforce the rules for themselves. Wilson suggests that these types of game are interesting because they encourage physical and social play to come to the fore of the gaming experience, as a result of the 'messy hybrid analog-digital' nature of the games. Considering games such as these is important when we are thinking about how attention is distributed and managed in digital play environments, because they challenge our common impressions of what digital play involves.

METHODS

Wilson centres his article around a case study of a game that he designed called Brutally Unfair Tactics Totally Ok Now (BUTTON). In this case, 2–8 players have to race towards the game controls, trying to get to them first in order to press a button that is shown on the screen. The players are each represented by a fantastical avatar, and for each turn, the winning avatar does a little dance to celebrate their victory. BUTTON is distinct from traditional videogames in that it leaves a lot of space for the players to work out how the game should be played together. The name of the game itself invites players to engage in 'brutal tactics', so that it encourages rough and tumble play to take centre stage – not something we typically associate with computer gaming. Wilson reflects on the game design and the experiences he has observed of participants playing the game in different social settings.

FINDINGS

Wilson suggests that 'broken' games such as BUTTON encourage players to work together, improvising and negotiating the nature of the game play as they go along. He describes this as a 'design it yourself spirit' and suggests that it 'supports a distinctly self-motivated and collaborative form of play'. How attention is managed in this kind of physical–digital environment is completely different from how attention is managed in a 1–1 gaming environment, for example where a player is alone with the screen and essentially

(Continued)

playing 'against the computer'. Because the physical and social dimensions of the digital play are so important in a game such as BUTTON, attention will need to be distributed between these different aspects of the situation, for example with players' attention more on each other than on the screen display. The case study of BUTTON also highlights that we need to remember that the pace in digital gaming can come from the players as much as from the digital visual display. Often when we consider digital play environments, we assume that the pace of the play stems from how quickly the visual display switches, but in alternative gaming environments, the rapid pace stems from the competitive and collaborative interactions between players.

REFLECTION ACTIVITIES

- Explore the experience of playing some alternative independent games that rely on a 'digital craft' aesthetic. Lumino City is a great place to start. What are your impressions of the game? How is it the same as/different from other more popular forms of digital game-playing?

- If possible, play this kind of game with a child. After the experience, jot down your notes about the experience. Did you enjoy it? Did the child seem to enjoy playing this game? What was enjoyable about it? Did you miss the pace that is typical of more traditional videogames?

- If you can't download the app to play yourself, you can access it on YouTube videos of other users playing the game so that you get a good idea of what the game looks and feels like. Watch the video and consider the questions above in relation to what you saw.

CHAPTER SUMMARY

- Psychologists suggest that shifts in cognitive processing have occurred as a result of our frequent engagement with digital technologies. For example, they suggest that we generally process information more shallowly and that we are more reliant on external memory stores (e.g. photographs, or the internet).

- Whether these shifts in cognitive style are maladaptive (i.e. whether they are unhelpful to us) depends on the context in which we are operating. They may be beneficial when we are engaging in our lives at home but maladaptive in traditional classrooms, where deeper information processing and internal memory are still valued.

- Some researchers – most notably Susan Greenfield – have argued that there is a causal link between our frequent engagement with digital technologies and the increasing diagnoses of attention deficit and hyperactivity disorder (ADHD).

- In relation to these claims, we need to remain aware that most of the data used to support the claims come from studies of adolescents and adults, rather than young children. We also need to consider other explanations for the increase in ADHD diagnoses, such as the potential mismatch between children's home lives and what is expected of them when they go to school.

- There is a common perception that videogames are fast-paced and do not enable calmer exploration. However, there is a whole other genre of games (sometimes called 'digital craft' or 'post-digital games') that encourage slowed-down investigations of alternative worlds. These facilitate a slower form of engagement and may even encourage the immersive pleasure state that Denmead and Hickman (2012) term 'slowliness'.

RESEARCH ACTIVITIES

- Carry out your own version of the Brasel and Gips study on media multi-tasking (see first Research Spotlight in this chapter). In this study, adult participants were observed as they browsed a computer and also watched television. You could conduct this study, but with younger children as the participants. Have the television on in the background and then give them a tablet, phone or computer to play on at the same time. Based on a video observation, count how many times their gaze switches between the television and the alternative device. What does this suggest about the division of their attention? If you had the time and resources, you could even conduct this study comparing the behaviour of children and adult participants. Do children or adults do more attention-switching when they are engaged in media multi-tasking?

- Interview or survey teachers, parents and/or children about their thoughts on the relationship between digital technologies and ADHD. Is digital engagement really to blame for the rise of ADHD? How convincing do your participants find this argument? Do they think other factors might be important?

- Conduct observations of a child (or children) engaging with a 'digital craft' game such as Lumino City and Minecraft. If possible, capture the observation through video. Based on the observation, reflect on the experience that these sorts of game enable. Was participation thoughtful, slowed down and more deliberate than you would expect when videogaming? Did you observe any behaviours that are indicative of 'slowliness' (an immersive pleasure state based on sensory exploration)? If possible, interview the player after the experience. How did they find it? Did they enjoy it? What did they enjoy about the experience?

FURTHER READING

- Mavoa, J., Gibbs, M., & Carter, M. (2017). Constructing the young child media user in Australia: A discourse analysis of Facebook comments. *Journal of Children and Media, 11*(3), 330–346.

In this research study, Mavoa et al. explore the discourses shared by practitioners online about digital technologies in education. They show that there are often negative discourses suggesting that children are 'losing out' as a result of the integration of digital technologies into education, though this is typically not supported with research evidence.

- Robinson, K. (2010). Changing education paradigms. *TED Talk*. Available at: www.ted.com/talks/ken_robinson_changing_education_paradigms (accessed 29 January 2019).

In this talk, Ken Robinson argues that our modes of education are outdated and that this is part of the reason why diagnoses for ADHD among children have risen. He suggests that it is the way we educate children that needs to change – bringing it in line with the rest of children's experiences – rather than worrying that children themselves are 'going wrong'.

- Wilson, J. (2005). Indie rocks! Mapping independent video game design. *Media International Australia incorporating Culture and Policy, 115*(1), 109–122.

Wilson offers a helpful analysis of the independent games industry, giving an insight into alternative genres of videogaming that can challenge our common perceptions of what digital play involves. As Wilson shows, there are lots of types of digital gaming experience that do not conform to the same expectations of the most popular games. We can gather from Wilson's analysis inspiration in relation to thinking about opportunities for children's digital play that go beyond the 'norm'.

8

DIGITAL PLAY AND A CHILD'S SENSE OF SELF

INTRODUCTION

This chapter focuses on the contribution of digital play to children's emerging sense of who they are – their Self. In this chapter we will:

- explore how the Self develops through our relationships with others, and comes about through dialogues and participation in particular groups. We consider how digital play can enable particular dialogues between family members, but also outside of families, which feed into a child's sense of who they are;
- examine self-presentation activities that are encouraged in digital environments. Self-presentation involves creating a public Self that we develop and share primarily for the consumption of others. Digital environments, particularly social media, are strongly associated with the practices of self-presentation;
- examine the distinction between self-presentation and self-representation. While self-presentation relates to the creation of a public Self for others, self-representation relates to the processes through which we make sense of who we are – self-discovery and self-transformation. We explore how digital environments may sometimes actually facilitate self-representation, even when it seems as though they are more likely to support self-presentation.

Much of the research conducted into self-making in digital environments has been conducted with adolescents and adults, though some key studies have been conducted with younger children. This means that while we can relate the research that has been done with older individuals to our understanding of digital play in early childhood, we need to do this with caution and keep in mind how activities might be different from a child's perspective. Further research is required to understand more specifically about children's sense of self in relation to digital play, and through this chapter you will find observations, Research Spotlights and Reflection Activities that focus more explicitly on experiences in early childhood. At the end of the chapter, suggested Research Activities give you an opportunity to contribute to this under-developed area of research.

CASE STUDY 8.1

PERSONALISED STORY-MAKING

M (4 years old) and her father are playing with the app 'Mr Glue' on an iPad together. In Mr Glue, users can personalise storybooks by choosing the names of characters, selecting particular elements in the story such as the setting, making audio recordings of sound effects to accompany the story, and drawing pictures that go with the story. At this point in the observation, M and her father have chosen the main protagonist in the story to be called 'Daddy'. They decided another character – a character who will eventually rescue the protagonist – would be called 'Hannah', which is the name of M's best friend at school.

At this point in the observation, D is reading the personalised story out loud and M is laughing because she finds it funny that Hannah is rescuing 'Daddy'.

M: He keeps on saying daddy because he typed in daddy, because it's daddy and me doing it, but we just typed in daddy. And then it keeps on saying daddy . . . daddy shouted out for Hannah . . . daddy did this daddy did that . . . He's not even a kid!

[D continues reading out loud]

M: [interrupting]: and Hannah isn't even his friend; Hannah isn't his friend [M laughs] She's my friend

[M continues laughing while D reads out loud]

M: I put in Hannah and Hannah isn't even daddy's friend

D: I'm now on an adventure with your friend from school and I'm getting rescued by a five year old

[M laughs again]

THE SELF IN RELATION TO OTHERS

As much as we might think about the 'Self' as an individual phenomenon, it comes about through social experience and relationships with others. How we think about our Self and how we present our Self to others depends on our socialisation. This is demonstrated in research conducted by Bosacki, Varnish and Akseer (2008), which showed that how children draw themselves playing depends on their gender. Girls were more likely to show themselves engaged in social play, while boys were more likely to show themselves engaged in physical play. Gender is one factor in our lives that shapes how we think about our Self and how we share this with others, but there are many others – religion, culture, ethnicity, class and so on – that all influence our construction of the Self. Dialogues in the family have a particularly important role in shaping a child's sense of Self. It is likely that you will think about who you are in relation to others in your family, for example the ways in which you are similar to or different from your siblings (Bohanek, Marin, Fivush & Duke, 2006).

When thinking about digital play and engagement, one question we need to ask is how these dialogues and narratives that shape a child's sense of Self are manifesting in a digital environment. One exciting development is the prevalence of digital environments for children that enable personalisation, and which can therefore help children to make sense of who they are in relation to others. We can see this in the observation above, where the child is making sense of who is important to her by naming characters in the story. She is exploring power relations through the relationships between characters, for example finding it funny when her father is rescued in the story by her best friend Hannah, who is also a 5 year old. Research by Kucirkova et al. (Kucirkova, Messer, Sheehy & Flewitt, 2013; Kucirkova, Messer & Sheehy, 2014) demonstrates how powerful these personalised story-making apps can be for inviting dialogues between children and parents that in turn help a child to make sense of who they are and what matters to them. Family dialogues that influence a child's sense of Self are nothing new, but digital play can offer new opportunities for these interactions to occur.

Beyond the immediate family, other researchers suggest that digital play can open up new communities of participation to young children and these can become influential in terms of how children think about their Self. Dodge et al. (2008) observed 9–12-year-old children's engagement in a digital game called Quest Atlantic. They considered how the users found affinity groups in these online spaces, meaning groups of other users who they felt connected with and through whom they could develop a stronger sense of their own identity. The game was 'meaningfully appropriated and used in very different ways by each of the children' (p. 244), enabling them to explore aspects of what the researchers describe as their 'transactive self' (p. 227) – a term that highlights how our sense of Self exists and develops through our relationships with others.

RESEARCH SPOTLIGHT

Bassiouni, D.H., & Hackley, C. (2016). Video games and young children's evolving sense of identity: A qualitative study. *Young Consumers, 17*(2), 127–142.

AIMS

This research was an exploration of children's engagement with videogames in order to understand more about how this engagement might feed into children's emerging sense of identity. The researchers were interested in how videogaming might be a cultural resource for children as they navigate their identity in relation to others, including peers and their family.

METHODS

The research involved individual and group semi-structured interviews with 22 children aged between 6 and 12 years old. The researchers also gathered informal conversations with parents through an after-school club attended by the children. They recorded these informal exchanges and their own impressions of the situation in fieldnotes, which were part of the data analysis along with the interview transcripts. The researchers thematically analysed the data.

FINDINGS

The researchers found that the videogames were a shared cultural reference point that was important for the children when it came to forging a sense of who they were. The videogames were particularly important in acting as an identifier of group membership. By playing particular games, children felt that they were gaining access to a particular group identity. This was a gendered phenomenon, whereby boys placed more of an emphasis on videogames as a way to establish and make sense of their relationship with the peer group. In the context of the family, videogames were a route through which children could act autonomously. Their decision to play particular games, and their requests for parents to buy them particular games, was a way for children to feel that they had a distinctive identity within the family context.

REFLECTION ACTIVITIES

- Bassiouni and Hackley suggest that videogames are a source of identity for many children, helping children to make sense of who they are and how they are distinct from other members of the family. Does this resonate with your own experience? Can you think of a child you know for whom videogaming is an important source of identity and autonomy within the family?

- Explore a personalised story-making app with a child. 'Our Story', produced by the Open University, is a free app that enables users to put together photographs, videos, audio recordings and written captions in order to create stories about anything you like. This is a good app to use with a child to see how these platforms might offer opportunities to share narratives about everyday experience, which in turn can offer children the chance to make sense of who they are. After using the app with a child, jot down some notes about the experience. Were there opportunities for the child's self-exploration as a result of using the app? If so, what were these?

CASE STUDY 8.2

POSING FOR PHOTOGRAPHS

An extended family engage in a WhatsApp conversation. The grandchildren in the extended family, aged between 2 and 8 years, are often photographed by the parents and these photographs are shared around. One parent is sharing photographs of the family on holiday. Many of the photographs are of the children posing in different locations. One shows the 8-year-old girl in the family posing next to a large statue; she is leaning back and pouting in a posture often assumed by models. The grandmother in the family replies within the WhatsApp conversation: 'I'm not sure about this provocative pose!'

SELF-PRESENTATION

The term 'self-presentation' relates to activities through which we create and share a public Self – a version of ourselves that we send out into the public domain for the consumption of others (Nelson, Hull & Roche-Smith, 2008). When we think about digital engagement, particularly engagement in social media sites, self-presentation comes to the fore. For example, Arvidsson, Caliandro, Airoldi and Barina (2016) explore how individuals online can begin to think about themselves as micro-celebrities (Senft, 2008) and as part of this they engage in the 'staging of selfhood' (p. 933). Abidin (2017) considers how families, including young children, can be drawn into these activities of self-presentation, which often involve constructing a sense of 'authenticity' by portraying children and families engaged in everyday and mundane activities. In 'domestic filler' vlogs, for example, family influencers offer their digital audience insights into the family's developmental milestones, occasions and even how they go about doing their errands.

Abidin describes these online vlogs as examples of 'calibrated amateurism' – a term that relates to the presentation online of people's lives in such a way that we feel we are getting an insight into their private life, but really the whole presentation is staged. This builds on Goffman's (1959) notion of the 'staged backstage', which relates to situations in which individuals suggest that they are sharing more of their private selves than they normally would, but really they are carefully controlling what they share and how it makes others think about them. Many researchers suggest that social media sites encourage us to engage in 'self-conscious commodification' (Marwick & boyd, 2011a: 119), essentially constructing and selling an identity that we think others want to buy into. Perhaps this helps to explain the photograph shared in the WhatsApp group described in the observation above. The 8-year-old girl, but also her parents, are constructing an image of the Self that is intended for public consumption. The pose adopted by the girl suggests that there is self-consciousness in the construction of the photograph. On the other hand, the girls' Self is not being 'sold' to anyone in the extended family; indeed, her grandmother is disapproving of the photograph and shares this publicly.

RESEARCH SPOTLIGHT

Magnusson, L.O. (2018). Photographic agency and agency of photographs: Three-year-olds and digital cameras. *Australasian Journal of Early Childhood*, 43(3), 34–42.

AIMS

The research investigated 3 year olds' engagement with digital cameras in a preschool. The researcher was interested in how children's photography interacts with power relations in the preschool. Magnusson sought to explore how the spontaneous photographs of the children offered insights into the 'visual voices of the children' (p. 35), so that as adults we can better understand the children's experiences and perspectives.

METHODS

The research was conducted in two preschools working with two groups of 3 year olds: 26 children in total. The children in these settings were provided with cameras over a 3-week period by the researcher. They were not instructed how to use the cameras and took photographs spontaneously over the course of the day whenever they wished. They collectively produced 2200 photographs. The researcher observed the children as they went about their everyday learning experiences, including engagement with the cameras, and gathered over 70 hours of video observations of the children. The analysis was applied to both the video observations and the photographs taken by the children. Magnusson describes her approach to analysis as 'diffractive analysis', drawing on the new materialist approach of Barad (2007). In diffractive analysis, research is non-linear and exploratory; the researcher weaves their way through the data and theory, constructing an argument on the basis of this free-flow and playful process.

FINDINGS

The researcher shares photographs and explores how they 'visualise narratives about being a child in preschool' (p. 38). In this sense, the photographs offer insights into how the children see the world and how they experience their everyday realities in the preschool. The photographs shared and described by Magnusson are noticeably outward-looking. Rather than 'selfies', the children's photographs are relational – engaging with other children or adults in the preschool, and showing encounters with the material world around them. This suggests that the photography is a way of making sense of experiences, rather than being used to actively construct and present a Self. While there are concerns, often reported in popular media, that digital technologies and digital photography in particular are encouraging children to become obsessed with their own self-image, this research suggests that 3 year olds use digital photography to engage with the world around them and reflect on their connectedness. Beyond just insights into experience, the photographs – according to Magnusson – are powerful in the way that they lead to questions about the children's experience, and particularly the power structures that work on their experiences. This shows how digital photography, contrary to popular opinion, can be an exciting way to challenge social relationships and structures, and does not necessarily lead to children's 'self-presentation'.

REFLECTION ACTIVITIES

- Some researchers suggest that children's engagement with digital media encourages their narcissism and self-obsession, because social media platforms encourage us to 'stage' our lives and our sense of our lives for the consumption of others. Other researchers, such as Hess (2015), suggest that it is more complicated than this and that actually 'staging the self' (e.g. through selfies) can actually be more about connecting with others than about narcissism. What are your thoughts on this debate? Do you think digital media encourages or indulges narcissism, or do you think it enables connection, or is it capable of doing both?

- Explore the online profiles of 'family influencers'. In Abidin's article (outlined in the 'Further reading' section of this chapter), she explores how children are presented in the context of 'family influencers' who vlog about family life. Explore the online presence of these families for yourself and write down some of your immediate impressions. Do you think it's all 'a bit of fun' or do you think there is anything more sinister going on here in relation to children's sense of identity and privacy in the world?

> ## CASE STUDY 8.3
>
> ### A CONVERSATION IN SELFIES
>
> The day starts with a tearful goodbye between a mother and her 3-year-old daughter. The mother is going to work for the day, but the girl isn't happy about it. She repeats over and over, 'Mummy, I don't want you to go to work!'. The mother cuddles her child and says soothingly, 'Don't worry, shall I send you a picture of me on the bus?'. The girl nods and stops crying, though she still looks glum. As soon as the mother gets on the bus, she remembers to snap a picture of herself, which clearly shows the empty seats on the bus behind her and the hand rails. She doesn't bother to brush her hair or fix her make-up since the photograph is for her daughter; the most important thing – she thinks – is just to smile lots! She sends the photograph through to the children's nanny, who is at home looking after the children. An hour or so later, the mother receives a message from the nanny which repeats what the daughter said when she saw the photograph on the bus, and also then sends through some photographs of the daughter who is now playing happily in the garden. Over the course of the day, the girl (via the nanny) and the mother exchange a series of photographs and messages. The mother takes a series of selfies showing her doing different things over the course of the day – first on the bus, then in the office, and then in a classroom with her students. In each example, she takes little care over her appearance (except to make sure she has a big smile) and she makes sure that the physical environment and context are apparent through the photograph.

SELF-REPRESENTATION

As opposed to self-presentation, which we considered in the previous section of the chapter, self-representation relates to the potential for some activities to be about exploring and sharing the Self in a way that goes beyond just selling a Self that appears desirable to others (Nelson et al., 2008). For example, when we engage in an activity like journaling, we are exploring what it means to be who we are and how we fit into the world around us; this is self-representation rather than self-presentation. Some researchers have explored how these practices of self-representation might be carried out in digital and online spaces. For example, Zhao and Zappavigna (2018) have explored how digital scrapbooks can be used by women to 'curate the self'. Through digital scrapbooks, women can make the mundane details of their lives more meaningful – the ordinary becomes the extraordinary. Although these studies have primarily related to the practices of adults online, there are some examples from research of children also engaging in 'self-curating' through online engagement. Björkvall and Engblom (2010), for example, mapped the collection and curation of online images by children in a classroom, finding that these images were a way of making sense of the world and their own identity in it.

Some activities that we immediately associate with self-presentation – such as selfies – can be reconceptualised as self-representation. Hess (2015) suggests that although it is tempting to see selfies as the epitome of narcissism, they are actually more complex and exciting than this. Hess suggests that selfies are at the 'nexus of the intimate self, public spaces, locative technology and digital social networks' (p. 1630). Rather than being about selling our public image, they relate more often to the need for 'fleeting connection with others' and the 'compulsion to document ourselves in spaces and places' (p. 1631). We can see this in the observation that begins this section of the chapter. The mother is using selfies as a way to stay emotionally connected with her daughter who is struggling with separation anxiety. The selfies are not about presenting a desirable public Self, but rather about sharing her working day with her daughter for the sake of reassurance.

SELFIES: SELF-PRESENTATION OR SELF-REPRESENTATION?

In Figure 8.1, you can see two young cousins (5 and 8 years old) taking a selfie together on the 8-year-old's smartphone. The older cousin is taking the lead, but both children are familiar with the format of the selfie and how to pose, for example. When looking at an image like this, in order to determine whether it is more a practice of self-presentation or self-representation, we need to ask many questions about the particular context in which this selfie is taken. For example, we might ask the following:

1. What are the children going to do with the selfie once they have taken it?
2. Who else is going to see the selfie in the immediate social environment?
3. Are they going to send the selfie to others?
4. Are they going to share the selfie more publicly or is it just for close friends and family?
5. Are they going to edit the selfie at all? If so, what are the functions of the editing process? If they are planning to edit the photograph to make it look silly or funny, might this be more about bonding with each other than appearing in a particular way to others? Are they going to edit the photograph in order to achieve a particular self-image, or to look like other selfies that they have seen?
6. Will they return the selfie at a later date? If so, what for? Will the selfie represent a shared memory between the cousins?

Figure 8.1 Two young cousins taking a selfie together

RESEARCH SPOTLIGHT

Park, C.S., & Kaye, B.K. (2018). Smartphone and self-extension: Functionally, anthropomorphically, and ontologically extending self via the smartphone. *Mobile Media & Communication 7*(2), 215–231. Available at: https://journals.sagepub.com/doi/abs/10.1177/2050157918808327.

AIMS

This study is an investigation into the boundaries that exist between the 'human self' and the digital technologies that we use, particularly our smartphones. It explores how those boundaries can become blurred as smartphones play an increasing role in our lives. The research builds on ideas of the 'extended self' – a concept introduced by Russell Belk in 1988. In this concept, the self is not seen as something confined to the human body, but extends to resources that we use as part of our everyday lives.

METHODS

The researchers conducted in-depth interviews with 60 heavy smartphone users. The interviewees on average used their smartphone for 4 hours and 23 minutes a day. The interviews were semi-structured and lasted about an hour each. The researchers transcribed the interviews and conducted a deductive thematic analysis, exploring comments in relation to three categories of the 'extended self' that they introduce in the background of the article: 1) the functional self, 2) the anthropomorphic self and 3) the ontological self. These categories of extended self are explained and illustrated in the section below.

FINDINGS

The researchers related the interviewee responses to three types of 'extended self'. Firstly they noted examples of 'functional extended self'. This related to the individuals using their smartphones as a way to enhance their capabilities. For example, many of the interviewees talked about the integral role of the smartphone in managing their schedules. Secondly, the researchers found examples of 'the anthropomorphic extended self', whereby users conceptualise and interact with their smartphone as if it were a social entity. They talk about having a 'special relational bond' (p. 218) with the smartphone. For one interviewee, the smartphone in this sense was an integral part of her sense of self; she explained 'My smartphone is like my avatar. It tells me who I am' (p. 222). Thus, the smartphone is both a social 'other' that users have a relationship with, but also an essential part and symbol of identity. Finally, the researchers focused on examples of 'ontological extended self', which is when users feel that they do not have control over the smartphone, but instead the smartphone is a part of who they are and the lives they lead whether they like it or not. This relates to examples where the users feel that the smartphone is 'disrupting balance and interrupting mental flow' (p. 219). Some interviewees discussed how their emotional states would fluctuate depending on their engagement with the smartphone, or if they were separated from the smartphone. Together, the in-depth findings from this study demonstrate how the smartphone can be seen as part of the 'extended self' and that this has both negative and positive consequences for individuals' sense of self and wellbeing.

REFLECTION ACTIVITIES

- According to Bruner, Lucariello and Nelson (1989), self-making begins very early in childhood. In Nelson's research, an 18 month old was observed constructing their self through their self-directed talk at bedtime. If you have the opportunity to observe young children, make a note of instances where they are constructing their sense of self. This might be through language or through other modes, such as through photographs.

- In research by Park and Kaye (2018; see Research Spotlight), adults' smartphones are associated with three types of self-extension: functional self-extension, anthropormophic self-extension and ontological self-extension. Check that you understand the definitions of each type of self-extension, and now consider your own use of your smartphone in relation to these. Which types of self-extension apply to your own patterns of use?

CHAPTER SUMMARY

- The Self exists in relation to others and is made through the process of socialisation. Day to day, the child's sense of Self emerges through dialogues with others and particularly through family narratives. When we think about digital play, particularly personalisation in digital environments, we see that there are new opportunities for families to engage in dialogues and narrative-making that feeds into a child's sense of Self.

- Digital play online enables access to new affinity groups for children. Through participation in these groups, children have the opportunity to build a sense of Self that is distinct from their relationships with families and immediate peer relationships.

- The term 'self-presentation' is used to describe activities in which we create and promote a public Self. Many researchers suggest that social media encourages self-presentation. Although children are too young to have their own profiles on the most popular social media sites, children still have a presence in these online spaces, for example through the phenomenon of 'family influencers'.

- Self-representation (as opposed to self-presentation) occurs when we engage in activities through which we can explore and discover our sense of who we are. There are many examples of digital engagement that can be seen as activities of self-representation, for example digital scrapbooking. Even selfies – which are often understood as examples of self-presentation – can be seen again through the lens of self-representation.

RESEARCH ACTIVITIES

- Explore how children's sense of self is developed through selfies. For this Research Activity, you will need to work with one or more children over the course of at least a whole day. You might do this with children in a nursery/school setting, or you might do this with children who you know informally – for example through your family. Over the course of the day, observe how children use selfies and how these selfies might feed into their self-construction and emerging sense of self. Selfies will not necessarily be part of the children's everyday activities already, in which case you will want to get them into the habit of taking selfies at the start of the day, and over the course of the day, the children can take an increasing lead in choosing when and where to take the selfies. Over the day, note down how selfies are used by the children and by you. Use the questions when, what, why, who, where and why to explore the role of selfies in children's everyday life. Return to the debate discussed in the section of this chapter entitled 'Self-presentation' (p. 115). Do your observations of how selfies are used relate to the idea that this is an

> activity that encourages narcissism, or did you observe selfies more often being used to connect with others and to centre the self in time and place?
>
> - Perhaps with the same group of children, explore the role of personalised narratives through digital media in constructing the Self. Using the app 'Our Story' (or something similar), create – together with children – narratives about everyday life and experiences, using photographs, audio recordings, videos and written captions. Reflect afterwards on how the children engaged with the app – what narratives did they want to capture and explore? How did these narratives relate to their sense of self and their connections with others? Was there anything that this activity gave them in terms of sense of self that other non-digital activities might not allow for?

FURTHER READING

- Hess, A. (2015). The selfie assemblage. *International Journal of Communication*, 9(18), 1629–1646. Available at: https://ijoc.org/index.php/ijoc/article/viewFile/3147/1389.

Hess explores how we think about selfies and their role in our everyday lives. He argues that while it can be tempting to see selfies as an act of narcissism and self-obsession, selfies are actually more complex than this. They are also about connecting with others, and about 'touching down' in the particular times and places that make up our everyday lives. This article helps to open up our thinking about common forms of digital engagement that might look like self-presentation on first impressions, but may actually involve more self-representation than we expect.

- Kucirkova, N., Messer, D., Sheehy, K., & Flewitt, R. (2013). Sharing personalised stories on iPads: A close look at one parent–child interaction. *Literacy*, 47(3), 115–122.

In this article, Kucirkova et al. (2013) report a small-scale research study that involved observing a mother and a young child creating a personalised story together on the iPad. They explore how this activity can facilitate closeness between the mother and the child as they reflect together on their everyday activities.

- Marwick, A., & boyd, d. (2011). To see and be seen: Celebrity practice on Twitter. *Convergence, 17*(2), 139–158.

In their research, Marwick and Boyd explore how adult celebrities use Twitter to create and grow their 'fan base'. They explore the particular practices that the celebrities engage in in order to create a sense of connection and a 'staged authenticity' that their followers will buy into. Although this research relates to adult users, the findings are fascinating in relation to the concept of 'self-presentation' and thinking about how digital environments, particularly social media sites, are changing how we think about the Self as an entity and what we do to share our Self with others. You might find it interesting to reflect on your own everyday use of social media in relation to the ideas introduced in this article.

9
DIGITAL PLAY IN CONTEXT

INTRODUCTION

In this chapter, we explore how the context that surrounds children's digital play shapes the phenomenon of digital play. This chapter:

- examines the role of the adult in relation to children's engagement in digital play, by considering research on the mediation and intermediation of children's digital play;
- analyses the dominant discourses that surround children's digital play and considers how these discourses contribute to your mediation practices as adults working or living with children;
- discusses the challenges of using the term 'digital play' when the boundaries between digital and non-digital environments are so blurred in children's play. We question whether the term 'digital play' should even be used at all.

In this chapter you will find observations, theoretical summaries, Research Spotlights and Reflection Activities that enable us to see digital play in its wider sociocultural context. In addition, we examine newspaper headlines as a way of making sense of the dominant discourses that surround children's digital play, and you are invited at the end of the chapter to conduct some of your own research – including your own discourse analysis – in order to gain a deeper understanding of digital play in context.

> **CASE STUDY 9.1**
>
> **ENGAGING WITH THE INTERACTIVE WHITEBOARD DURING FREE-FLOW ACTIVITY TIME**
>
> It is free-flow time in the reception classroom. There are many activities available to the 4–5 year olds in the classroom and outside, which is accessible through a door that is kept open. Different 'activity stations' are set up around the environment. The children have access to the Interactive Whiteboard (IWB) and a simple drawing app that is open on the IWB. The teacher and teaching assistant in the class are absorbed in other areas of the learning environment. At different points they are observing children at the 'writing' and 'counting' tables; they are also managing behaviour that they see as disruptive, and they are supervising the children who go outside. This means that there is little chance for them to interact with those children who have chosen to use the IWB. Having said this, there are physical clues placed next to the IWB which indicate to the children how they should be interacting with the IWB. For example, on the small table next to the IWB there is a sand-timer. The children tell each other when they are waiting for their turn: 'you've had your go, look at the sand-timer'. The children organise themselves quite rigidly around the IWB, for example queueing for their turn rather than attempting to use the IWB together. Even though the teachers are not immediately present, the teacher's presence can still be felt through the way the children police each other and ensure that turn-taking rules are followed.

MEDIATING DIGITAL PLAY

Research has repeatedly demonstrated a lack of proactive mediation by adults in early childhood settings when it comes to digital play. Plowman and Stephen (2005) found that practitioners are more likely to engage in 'reactive supervision' in relation to children's engagement with digital technologies. This means that the adults would only get involved when something had gone wrong, such as the technology breaking down, or a conflict emerging between children about who should be using the technology. Other types of mediation – such as co-playing, questioning or observing – were avoided by the practitioners observed as part of this study. Since this seminal research study, other researchers have noted a similar phenomenon (Edwards, 2016; Sakr and Scollan, 2019). Practitioners' reluctance to engage proactively is a response to a lack of confidence about their own digital capabilities, as well as a general scepticism around the value of digital play in children's lives (Sakr, 2017). These two factors – the lack of confidence and the scepticism – are, of course, intertwined. The more confident practitioners feel about engaging with digital environments, the more likely they are to come across forms of digital play that they believe to be beneficial for children. In response to practitioners' reluctance to engage with children's digital play in a proactive manner, Edwards (2016) developed the tool of web-mapping, in which the practitioner notes down how a child's passions and interests arise in different play environments (including digital environments). For example, a practitioner might be aware through a child's drawings that they are drawn to a particular digital environment that they play with at home. In order to enable the flow of ideas and activities, the practitioner might then be more inspired to bring that particular digital environment into the classroom and make it accessible to children as part of their free-flow activity time.

When we think about proactive or reactive mediation, we tend to think about what an adult is physically doing. However, mediation does not always involve the immediate presence of an adult. Sometimes it takes the forms of clues and cues in the physical environment that are designed (by adults) to shape how children take up and engage with digital media. Sakr and Scollan (2019; see Research Spotlight later in the chapter) explore how physical clues, like a sand-timer placed next to digital technologies in the learning environment, can indicate to children how they should be engaging in digital play. In the case of the sand-timer for example, children receive the message that their time is limited with these particular resources. Children are likely to pick up on this type of cue because the sand-timer marks out the digital technology as different from most other resources in the early years learning environment where no time limits are indicated. We are unlikely to find a sand-timer next to the drawing table or the sandpit, for example. So mediation is not just about what adults do as children engage with digital technologies, but also about how they construct the sociocultural and physical environment and the clues that are embedded in the environment as a result.

In addition to mediation, we need also to consider the role of intermediation in the context of children's digital play. Nansen and Jayemanne (2016) use the term 'intermediation' to describe how adults' practices construct particular discourses around children's digital engagement. Through intermediation adults develop and reinforce particular expectations around how children will engage with digital media, and this in turn shapes how adults think about and carry out mediation processes. In their study of YouTube videos of very young children interacting with the iPad, Nansen and Jayemanne show how such videos lead to the perception of the iPad as a 'natural' interface that young children are capable of immediately learning. Such a perception feeds into the conceptualisation of children as 'digital natives' (Prensky, 2001) who are capable of quickly picking up how to use digital technologies since they have never known life without digital technologies present.

The discourse of the 'digital native' has particular effects on how we then support (or do not support) children's digital technology use, for example if children are 'digital natives' there is no need for them to be explicitly shown how to use digital technologies at nursery or school. They are left 'to get on with it' ('reactive supervision') and the emphasis in formal educational settings is placed on activities that are thought to require more instruction (e.g. reading and writing). The 'digital native' discourse also creates a perception that all children have the same level of ability with digital media, when actually a significant body of research shows that the types of digital experiences that children are having at home depends a lot on their socio-economic status and the amount of time that their parents have to scaffold and support their digital play and learning experiences (Selwyn, 2009; Livingstone et al., 2015). Mediation and intermediation feed off of one another and we need to keep both processes in mind when thinking about the context of digital play and how to shape this context in order to best support the child.

RESEARCH SPOTLIGHT

Willett, R.J. (2015). The discursive construction of 'good parenting' and digital media – the case of children's virtual world games. *Media, Culture & Society, 37*(7), 1060–1075.

AIMS

Willett's research is an exploration of the discourses that surround websites aimed at children, and how parents are made to think about themselves in relation to the mediation of their children's digital engagement. Willett examines what discourses are constructed in the popular media around three popular websites for children (ClubPenguin, Poptropica and Minecraft) and how these discourses feed into parents' identities as 'good parents' whose primary role is to keep their children safe.

METHODS

Willett applies discourse analysis to coverage in popular UK and US media (newspapers and magazines) surrounding three popular websites for children. She also analyses the discourse (the text) that appears on these websites themselves, for example in the 'about us' section. Her analysis involved 236 articles about ClubPenguin, 64 articles about Poptropica and 60 articles about Minecraft. She identified recurrent themes in the discourse, which related to the role of these websites in keeping children safe in what is generally seen as a risky online context.

FINDINGS

Willett's discourse analysis demonstrates how websites targeted at children market themselves as 'safe' online spaces, and imply that the wider internet is a risky place with online 'stranger danger' that parents need to ensure that their children avoid. Through the popular discourses that surround these commercial websites, parents are made to feel that they are being 'good parents' by enabling their children access to these particular websites. They feel that they are good parents because they are keeping their children safe from other more risky online environments. Another aspect of the discourse surrounding these websites is the elision between play and learning, so that parents are invited to understand these websites as spaces for learning and 'not just play'.

REFLECTION ACTIVITIES

- Think about a setting that you have access to – maybe a nursery, school or a home setting. What mediation practices do you see going on in relation to children's digital engagement in this setting? How do adults in this setting structure and support children's digital play? Jot down all the instances of child–adult interaction that you see occurring in relation to children's digital play and then think about the type of mediation that this represents – maybe it's monitoring, or limiting, or supervising, or co-playing, and so on.

- Explore YouTube videos as a way to better understand the concept of 'intermediation'. Search for videos posted by parents showing their children interacting with different types of digital technology. What do the videos show about the children's engagement with digital media? Is it presented as 'something natural' that the child immediately 'gets'? What about the comments underneath the videos? How do they feed into the intermediation and the discourses that are being constructed about children's engagement with digital media?

MEDIA REPRESENTATION OF DIGITAL PLAY

Three recent newspaper headlines about children's digital engagement:

1. Digital footprint starts in the womb, Children's Commissioner warns
2. Digital media helps with parenting and brings families together
3. Young kids spend over 2 hours a day on screens

For each of these headlines, jot down your immediate impressions. What images come into your mind when you read the headline? What mood does the headline create? Do you feel positive/negative/neutral as you read the headline?

(Continued)

> Have a look again at the headlines below and this time focus particularly on the parts of the headline that have been underlined. How do these particular words or phrases contribute to your immediate impression of the headline? What perceptions about children's digital media engagement do these headlines respond to and reinforce?
>
> 1. Digital footprint starts in the womb, Children's Commissioner <u>warns</u>
> 2. Digital media <u>helps</u> with parenting and <u>brings families together</u>
> 3. Young kids spend <u>over 2 hours</u> a day <u>on screens</u>
>
> Here are some things you might have noticed as you look again at these headlines:
>
> - In the first headline, the word 'warns' suggests that this is a negative phenomenon. We might not assume that babies having a 'digital footprint' is necessarily a bad thing, but through the use of the word 'warns', the headline is suggesting that we should feel concerned about this situation.
>
> - The second headline is quite unusual because it highlights some of the positive aspects of children's digital media engagement as have been found through research. It is particularly unusual because it highlights the social dimension of digital media: the parents, and the whole family being supported. We might be less surprised to see a headline relating to advances in cognitive development as a result of digital engagement, but it is quite rare to find a headline reporting positively on the social consequences of children's digital media engagement.
>
> - At first, the third headline might look like it is quite a neutral statement; after all, it is remarking only on the amount of time that children are spending engaged with screen-based digital technologies. However, the phrase 'over 2 hours' implies that this is a large amount of time and that we should feel shocked by this. If the same findings were reported as 'under 3 hours', we would most likely feel the opposite – that actually children were not spending too much time with digital technologies at all. Also, the phrase 'on screens' is a catch-all term that conjures up the image of a child fixated on a screen. If instead we used the term 'engaging in digital play', our perceptions would likely be different since the 'play' is something we think about as fun and active, and the verb 'engaging' suggests that children are choosing what to do and they are active rather than passive.

CHALLENGING POPULAR DISCOURSES SURROUNDING CHILDREN'S DIGITAL PLAY

How we perceive and manage digital play as individuals will depend on the wider social context, and how digital play is talked and thought about more generally. How we talk and think about a particular phenomenon is known as a 'discourse' (Cameron, 2001). In the headlines above, we can see particular discourses at work – particular ways of thinking about and talking about digital play. For example, we can see the dominant discourse (that children's digital engagement is something that we need to be concerned about) in the first and third headline. The second headline is unusual in that it positions digital play as a positive influence on social interaction and family closeness, and so this headline is challenging the dominant discourse. It belongs to its own discourse (that we should be optimistic about the role of digital media in children's lives), but this discourse is less represented in the popular media.

Research suggests that practitioners in early childhood education are strongly influenced by the dominant discourses that surround children's digital media engagement. For example, Mavoa et al. (2017) conducted research analysing practitioners' comments on Facebook about children's interactions with digital technologies. They were interested in how these comments fed into a particular set of discourses about children's digital engagement. They found that there was a common thread in the comments that positioned children's digital engagement as a 'loss'. The comments showed that the practitioners were worried that children were losing their eyesight, losing opportunities to play outdoors, losing their imagination, and in a much more general sense, losing out on a 'proper childhood'.

Discourses surrounding children's engagement in digital play can also serve commercial purposes. In the discourse analysis of Willett (2015), she examines how discourses of 'good parenting' in relation to children's engagement with digital media are constructed through particular commercial websites designed for children (see the Research Spotlight earlier in the chapter). These particular websites present themselves and are reported in popular media as less risky alternatives to whatever else is available on the internet to be found and used by children. This creates and feeds into a discourse of 'risk' associated with children's digital play. In ClubPenguin's presentation of itself, for example, as primarily a 'safe space' for children to play in, the implication that parents take away is that beyond this designated safe space, the internet is a scary place for their children. In response to this, parents see their primary role as keeping their children safe by being selective about the environments through which their children engage in digital play.

Discourses shape how we mediate children's digital play. If we buy into the discourse of 'loss', for example, in relation to digital play, then we are unlikely to be fully supportive of children's engagement with digital play. We will automatically think about digital play as something that we need to limit in order to protect children's childhood. If we think about our own role as a supportive adult as primarily one that involves limiting screen time, then this will constrain greatly the types of support that we can actually offer to children while they play via digital technologies. If we are obsessing about time limits, and when we should 'cut the power', then we are likely to show a lower level of interest in what is actually happening in the digital play, and we are unlikely to allow ourselves to be drawn into co-playing (Squire & Steinkuehler, 2017).

As a result of this fundamental relationship between discourse and mediation, we – as adults working and/or living with children – need to actively disrupt the popular discourses that surround digital play. Instead of reacting to the perceived threat or loss posed by children's growing interest in digital play, we instead need to become deeply curious about it, ready to observe closely, and excited about the prospect of digital co-playing. If we are mindful enough to stop the flow from popular discourse into practitioner discourse, we can be open to the new possibilities of digital play and to constructing forms of digital play that do not look like all the worst case scenarios we typically come across in the newspaper headlines. For example, my research shows that digital play is often perceived by practitioners as negative as a result of 'sensory loss' (Sakr, 2017). Early years practitioners worry that digital creativity does not involve the highly sensory experiences that creating with non-digital resources involves. However, the phenomenon of 'makerspaces' is a direct challenge to this. In makerspaces, all sorts of resources are available – digital and non-digital. The aim is 'making', regardless of the resources that are chosen to be used, so that ideas flow between sticky Play-Doh and electronic circuits, or between gadgets that require hands-on coding and building blocks. Research exploring makerspaces in early childhood settings demonstrate how young children's play can be both digital and intense sensory experiences (Wohlwend, 2017b). When we see something like this in practice, we are less likely to hold onto the discourse of digital play as 'sensory loss' because we have engaged with an alternative possibility.

RESEARCH SPOTLIGHT

Gronn, D., Scott, A., Edwards, S., & Henderson, M. (2014). 'Technological me': Young children's use of technology across their home and school contexts. *Technology, Pedagogy and Education*, 23(4), 439–454.

AIMS

The researchers aimed to explore the lived realities of the hypothesised 'digital disconnect' between home and school. Much previous research has insisted that children experience a significant disconnect between their digital engagement at home (which tends to be led more by them and more frequent) and their digital engagement at school (which is thought to be more constrained). In this research study, Gronn et al. considered whether this digital disconnect can really be seen in the everyday experiences of young children and if so, what forms it takes.

METHODS

Gronn et al. conducted a study involving close observations of 12 children aged 2–12 years old. They observed these children as they engaged with digital technologies at home and in the school/nursery environment. For the sake of the article presented here, they focused in on data associated with just one family: three siblings aged between 5 and 12 years old. They tracked, through video recordings made by the siblings, the types of digital technologies they used in the home and school context, and the amount of time dedicated to these different types of use. They also conducted two focus group interviews with the three siblings to probe further into their experiences of digital engagement in both contexts, and the reasons underlying these forms of engagement.

FINDINGS

Close study of this particular family suggested that there were both similarities and differences in terms of how the children used digital technologies in the home and school contexts. While different technologies were used to different extents in both environments, digital engagement in both contexts appeared to be shaped by the same dominant purposes: information gathering and entertainment. While school did show a more constrained use of the internet, and more teacher-led activities, the children still used digital technologies at school for finding out particular things and for entertainment (e.g. as a reward given by the teacher). Based on these findings, the researchers suggest that rather than thinking about a 'digital disconnect', it is more appropriate to visualise the relationship between home and school in terms of digital technologies as 'a permeable boundary' (p. 444). Thus, children carry particular ways of thinking about and engaging with digital technologies across the transition from home to school, and back again.

REFLECTION ACTIVITIES

- Go online and find three recent headlines in the popular media that relate to children's engagement with digital technologies. What do the headlines suggest about how digital technologies are perceived? Is children's digital engagement positioned as something positive and exciting, or is it something that we need to be worried about? What discourses about digital media do the headlines contribute to?

- Think about a formal or informal setting for children who you have access to. It might be a nursery, playgroup, school or home environment. What are the dominant discourses about children's digital play in this particular setting? What would you do to 'shake up' these dominant discourses? For example, if the setting positions digital play as something that needs to be limited by adults, then what would happen if the time limits were removed for a week? How would this change the behaviours of both the children and the adults?

> **CASE STUDY 9.2**
>
> **PRACTISING YOUR SPELLINGS THROUGH A YOUTUBE SEARCH**
>
> Cousins (5-year-old S and 8-year-old M) are playing together one Sunday afternoon, using the internet-enabled television to find music videos and vlogs. M is chatting about the vloggers that she loves to watch on YouTube and what they do. S has just started to find videos for herself on YouTube and starts to spell out 'Hatchimals' in the YouTube search box. It takes some time for S to sound out the word and find the letters that she needs. M starts to intervene, thinking that she can find the video faster, but mum steps in: 'Oh don't M, she just needs a chance to do it, she's just learning to do it and it's good for her to practise.' A bit frustrated, M sinks back down onto the sofa and waits patiently for S to find what she is looking for. They start to play the video and S bounces up and down with excitement.

BLURRING THE BOUNDARIES

When we think about 'digital play' we tend to see it as something separate from other types or forms of play. Even the title of this book suggests that digital play is something specific with its own separate identity. Research suggests, though, that this is not the reality of children's everyday lived experiences. For them, their ideas and activities flow across different resources, digital and non-digital, and between different spaces. Even when we think that there might be a digital disconnect (e.g. between home and school), research suggests a higher than anticipated level of continuity in activities from the child's perspectives (see Research Spotlight above on Gronn et al., 2014).

The flow of practices across digital and non-digital environments has been emphasised by researchers approaching the issue from the perspective of new literacies. Researchers in this field tend to see children's literacy practices as fluid and multi-layered, and never just 'digital' or 'non-digital', but most likely both (Burnett et al., 2014; Burnett, Merchant, Simpson & Walsh, 2018). In the observation above of S, we can see the flow of literacy between different spaces (home and school) and via different resources, including both digital resources, such as the YouTube app on the Smart TV, and non-digital resources, such as the conversation between the two children, and the adult's involvement. This also links with the concept of connected play (Marsh, 2017) where children's play is observed moving back and forth between digital and non-digital environments, demonstrating how the distinction between these environments is perhaps more important in our own minds than it is in the actual experience of the child as it unfolds in their everyday context.

Furthermore, today's reality is that digital media are always part of the context, even when they are not tangibly present. Even when children are not given any digital technologies to play with, their role play may well feature digital technologies that are around them in their everyday experiences. You might well have observed a child pretending that they are interacting with their smartphone. Such observations emphasise the extent to which the digital is always at work in our wider sociocultural context, and since play is always influenced by the sociocultural context, it will always be entangled with digital technologies and digital media. Rather than 'digital play', perhaps all play is simply 'play in a digital context'. Following from this, we may need to change how we think about 'digital play'. Digital play is not a 'set' term with an established definition. Edwards (2013, 2016) and Marsh et al. (2016) have offered in-depth explorations of what this term might mean, what it should refer to and how we can think about it. Adults working with young children need their own working definition of what constitutes digital play and where we place the boundaries that help us to think about 'digital play' in a constructive way. This can only be a 'working definition', since our experiences are constantly emerging and these will greatly influence how we construct our notions of digital play.

RESEARCH SPOTLIGHT

Sakr, M. & Scollan, A. (2019) The screen and the sand-timer: The integration of the interactive whiteboard into an early years free-flow learning environment. *Journal of Early Childhood Research*. Available at: https://doi.org/10.1177/1476718X19851538

AIMS

This research study explores how children engage with the interactive whiteboard (IWB) when they have access to it during free-flow learning time. The study considers how the physical environment of the classroom, as well as the social messages that surround the IWB, shape how the children engage with the digital technology. The researchers are interested in how adult mediation can unfold in relation to children's digital engagement when the adults are not immediately present – so how the children pick up clues from the environment about how they should engage with digital technologies.

METHODS

The study was based on a week-long observation study of one classroom environment of 4–5 year olds. The children were observed as they engaged with the IWB during free-flow

(Continued)

learning time. The observations were captured on a hand-held videocamera. The principal researcher was a participant observer and would sometimes interact with the children during their engagement with the IWB. The video recordings that were gathered over the week were analysed with a particular focus on the ways in which children entered into or exited from their interaction with the IWB. The researchers created a catalogue of entry and exit types, and these were used as a stepping stone for understanding how the children's engagement with the IWB was shaped by the physical environment around them and the social messages that they had picked up implicitly and explicitly from the adults in the classroom.

FINDINGS

The researchers found that the children tended to see the IWB as an activity that should be completed independently. They often took a negative view of attempts to collaborate in using the IWB. Policing of the IWB led to children engaging in particular turn-taking behaviours that they had picked up from other experiences of engagement with limited resources, such as queueing. Although the children were not told explicitly to queue or have such a rigid approach to turn-taking, they had picked up from the sociocultural and physical contexts that this was the 'right way' to use the IWB. Clues in the physical environment, such as a sand-timer placed on a small table next to the IWB, gave children the impression that they should be careful to take turns individually. Additionally, adults – including the participant observer – issued warnings about not upsetting one another in how they used the IWB, and this was understood by the children as the need to take individual turns one after the other. The research study demonstrates how adults' mediation of spaces, both explicit and implicit mediation, can lead to unintended consequences. In this particular classroom, children were unlikely to collaborate with each other when using the IWB because of the emphasis they placed on turn-taking.

REFLECTION ACTIVITIES

- Have you come across any example of children's play where there was engagement with digital technologies even though there were no digital technologies present? This might be a role play you saw that involved a child pretending to use a smartphone, or children engaging in rough and tumble play while pretending to be characters from their favourite videogame. What examples can you think of?

- How do you think we should see digital play? Is it a separate type of play, or is it an umbrella term that can apply to lots of different types of play? Is it helpful to use the term at all or should we get rid of it? After all, when children engage in play that makes use of paper, we don't tend to call it 'paper play'. Is it equally strange to talk about 'digital play' as though it is something we need to isolate and think about separately?

CHAPTER SUMMARY

- Research involving observations in early childhood education settings suggests that practitioners tend to engage in 'reactive supervision' rather than proactively mediating children's digital play through questioning or co-playing, for example.

- Adults' mediation of digital play does not necessarily depend on the physical presence of an adult. The way an environment is set up will influence how children engage in digital play.

- As well as mediation, we need to consider the phenomenon of 'intermediation', which refers to the practices that adults engage in that reinforce particular perceptions of children's digital play. For example, parents 'intermediate' children's digital play through videos of their own children that they post on YouTube, which suggests that their young children are 'digital natives'.

- Discourses are ways of thinking and talking about a particular aspect of society. Dominant discourses that surround children's digital play tend to emphasise 'loss' (the idea that children are 'losing out' by engaging in digital play) and risk.

- Examining the discourses that surround digital play is important because discourses influence how we mediate and intermediate children's digital play. If we think that digital play causes children to lose out on a 'proper' childhood, we are less likely to want to be highly involved and encouraging in relation to children's digital play.

- When we think about play experiences from the perspective of the child, we see that there is typically a flow of ideas and activities between digital and non-digital resources. This causes us to question the term 'digital play', which suggests that this is a separate type of play that fulfils distinct roles in a child's life. Perhaps instead of 'digital play' we need to instead just think about 'play in a digital context'.

RESEARCH ACTIVITIES

- Carry out an action research study focused on the mediation practices that surround children's digital media engagement in a setting you have access to. In action research, the aim is to benefit those around us by researching what happens when we make a change that we think might be an improvement. In your chosen setting – which might be a formal or informal setting – observe closely the mediation practices that adults typically engage in around children's digital play. Based on what you observe, think about what next steps could be taken to move these mediation

(Continued)

practices forward, making them more proactive and less reactive. Ideally, you would do this brainstorming with others in the setting – with other practitioners if you are based in a formal setting, and with other family members if you are based in an informal setting. If possible, implement changes to your own mediation practices and encourage others to try out these changes as well. Observe what happens as a result of the changes in the mediation practices of the setting. A cycle for your action research project might look like this: 1 week for the initial observation, 1 week for brainstorming beneficial changes in mediation practices and supporting others to make these changes, and 1 week observing what happens following the change in mediation practices.

- Conduct your own discourse analysis focusing on ten newspaper articles about children's engagement with digital media. Search for the articles using particular search terms (e.g. children, digital, technologies, childhood). Once you have identified the articles, read them through and highlight keywords and phrases that feed into a particular perspective of digital play. Consider whether the words and phrases you have highlighted reinforce a positive, negative or neutral perception of digital play in childhood.

FURTHER READING

- Burnett, C., Merchant, G., Simpson, A., & Walsh, M. (2018). *The case of the iPad: Mobile literacies in education.* Singapore: Springer.

In this edited collection, many different contributors present their research on the iPad, in educational contexts, from a New Literacy Studies perspective. Most of the chapters demonstrate how meaning-making is something that moves between different types of environment, and how the boundaries are blurred between digital and non-digital environments for learning, play and literacy.

- Edwards, S. (2013). Digital play in the early years: A contextual response to the problem of integrating technologies and play-based pedagogies in the early childhood curriculum. *European Early Childhood Education Research Journal*, 21(2), 199–212.

Edwards questions how we think about digital play and how we can determine whether it counts as 'real' play. She shows that whether you think about digital play as real play will depend on your definition of play in general and that this is not the same for everyone. Edwards emphasises the way in which play enables children to become active participants in culture, and she suggests that on this basis we should definitely think about digital play as real play, since digital media offers children many ways to actively participate in and create the culture around them.

- Selwyn, N. (2009). The digital native – myth and reality. *Aslib Proceedings*, *61*(4), 364–379.

Selwyn's influential article challenges the conceptualisation of children as 'digital natives'. Prensky (2001) first introduced the idea of the 'digital native', and it has become a popular way of thinking about children's relationship with digital technologies. Selwyn's careful review of previous research demonstrates how children's engagement with digital media is much more complex than the 'digital native' concept suggests.

10

CONCLUSION

SHAPING THE FUTURE OF DIGITAL PLAY IN EARLY CHILDHOOD

In this final chapter, I want to spend some time with the themes that cut across all of the previous chapters and help us to think more generally about how we can shape the future of digital play in early childhood. This chapter:

- highlights the complexity of the digital play debate, which involves looking at digital play in the context of wider social trends, as well as looking at the complexity inherent in the term 'digital play';
- suggests possibility thinking as a proactive way of shaping the future of digital play. Possibility thinking enables us to critically examine the popular discourses that surround digital play and it also offers a strategy for creating new forms of digital play that resonate with all we believe to be important in the learning and wellbeing of young children;
- advocates a 'guerrilla design' approach, whereby we rely on our own imagination and whatever digital resources are freely or cheaply available in order to create new forms of digital play that suit the particular children we work or live with;
- outlines some next steps for supporting digital play in early childhood; this includes the urgent need for further research from various disciplinary perspectives and research paradigms, and a cultivation of creativity, curiosity and criticality among practitioners, facilitated by the institutions in which they work.

Although the chapter shares ideas about how we move forward, it is not a checklist. It focuses on the need to cultivate a particular attitude to digital play that hopefully you feel has resonated throughout all of the previous chapters. If you take one thing away from this chapter and even this book, I hope it will be the sense that early childhood practitioners are excellently positioned to make a huge difference to the future of digital play in early childhood, and that this contribution can be achieved through the 3Cs: creativity, curiosity and criticality.

DIGITAL PLAY: A DEBATE OF MANY LAYERS

As we have seen in the previous chapter, it can be tempting to get caught up in the popular discourses that surround digital play. These discourses tend to present digital play as highly contentious and essentially a risk to the current generation of children. We need to be aware though that, as with all media headlines, these discourses are partly constructed to capture our attention, and as a result, the issues are presented as more extreme and one-sided than they actually are. As adults caring for young children, we have a duty to take a step back and see the rise of digital play among young children in all its complexity, recognising the many layers that make up what is going on. We need to avoid reducing the debate to a simple distinction between 'good' and 'bad'.

The first aspect that we need to be aware of is that the rise of digital play has occurred amidst lots of other social changes that have affected childhood experiences. For example, commercialisation, globalisation, an emphasis on children's academic achievement, and fears about 'stranger danger' are all social forces that have changed children's play experiences over the last 20 years or so. This means that we need to be cautious about attributing shifts in children's play experiences solely to the rise of digital play. Social trends influencing childhood are all entangled, and we need to be careful not to isolate any one single element of the sociocultural landscape and turn this into a scapegoat for any of the wider concerns we have.

Take the example of outdoor play for example, which we looked at more closely in Chapter 3. Many popular commentators and even some academic researchers of play have positioned the rise of digital play and the decline of outdoor play side by side. As a consequence, digital technologies have been blamed for children not playing outside as much as they seem to have done in previous generations. However, when we conduct research with children and parents about the barriers to outdoor play, we see that there are many wider social trends that are important to consider, and it would be unfair to pinpoint all – or even a significant proportion of the blame – on digital play. As discussed in more detail in Chapter 3, research demonstrates that we need to consider parental perceptions of their children's safety during unsupervised outdoor play as the primary inhibitory factor in relation to children's outdoor play (O'Brien & Smith, 2002; Veitch et al., 2006; Witten et al., 2013). Indeed, one study with children conducted by

Brockman, Jago and Fox (2011) found that children owning mobile phones was actually supportive of children playing outdoors unsupervised, since parents felt able to contact their children via the phones and were therefore less worried about them going out unsupervised.

As discussed in Chapter 2, digital play has also been blamed for declining physical activity among children, and as explored in Chapter 7, digital play has been blamed for the increase in rates of ADHD diagnoses. The evidence underlying the blame approach in these situations is purely based on correlation – that is, that at the same time as these negative aspects of contemporary childhood have come to the fore in popular media, simultaneously we have seen the rise of digital engagement in childhood. Popular commentators quickly make the leap from correlation to causation, but there is little evidence to support the idea that digital play is causing these wider shifts in children's behaviours. There are many plausible alternatives that we need to thoroughly consider. Firstly, it is possible that the trends are shaped by another factor. For example, the difficulties that parents face in contemporary society to juggle the demands of childcare at home with paid work outside the home might be contributing to all of these shifts: the decline of outdoor play, children's physical inactivity, the rise of digital play and mental health struggles among children could all relate to the struggles for relaxed play time together in modern families. Another possibility is that there is a causal link between some of these factors, but that actually the causal relationship goes in the other way to what most popular presentations of the issue suggest – so that rather than blaming digital play for the decline of outdoor play, we might see the rise of digital play as a consequence of the difficulties of going outside to play. There is some evidence for this in the study conducted by Brockman et al. (2011), which found that children did indeed want to go outside to play, but that this was difficult for a range of reasons (mostly relating to safety and security), and as a result, children fell back on their engagement in digital play as an alternative way to spend free time.

In reality, it is most likely that all of these social trends are interwoven, and that the causal flows between different factors work in both directions depending on the specific situation. In the diagram below (Figure 10.1), you can see a network of the various social influences that are shaping children's contemporary experiences of play. Access to digital technologies is part of this network, but only part, and it interacts continuously with the other aspects of the network.

Another aspect of the debate's complexity is the multi-dimensional nature of 'digital play' itself. The term 'digital play' makes the phenomenon sound like something that is neat and tidy and can be measured. As discussed in the previous chapter though, and also explored in Chapter 1, observational research of children engaging with digital technologies as part of their play demonstrates that there really is nothing so neat about 'digital play'. This is because when we engage in digital technologies, we are very rarely completely absorbed in that specific digital environment. When children play,

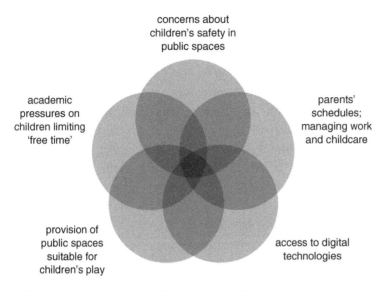

Figure 10.1 Trends in contemporary play as a network

they move across spaces and environments, and this means moving between digital and non-digital actions as part of 'connected play' (Marsh et al., 2016; Marsh, 2017). In connected play, there are aspects of children's play that make use of digital technologies, but there are also aspects of the play that are deeply connected to the physical world beyond the digital technology. For example, a child playing a game through an app on a phone might still be interacting socially with the people around them, or taking ideas from the app and enacting them as part of a role play, singing or dancing along to the music on the app and so on. The movement of ideas and actions across digital and non-digital environments can happen in the immediate moment of play, or they can happen across days, such as when children play together in the playground using the plots and characters from their favourite videogames as inspiration.

When we engage with the realities of connected play, it has an interesting effect on how we position the debate about the influences of digital play on children's lives. We start to see digital play as something that cannot be blamed because it is not really a single element or distinctive type of play. It has porous boundaries and is inevitably bound up, or entangled, in all other aspects of a child's life. In response to the tendency to position digital play and outdoor play in opposition to one another, thinking instead about 'connected play' enables us to realise the potentials of digital play that go beyond what we typically think of. For example, we are more likely to see the possibilities for digital play enabling children to become more active, or to develop a stronger connection with nature in their play, or engage intensively in social interactions with those immediately around them while playing through digital technologies.

POSSIBILITY THINKING AROUND DIGITAL PLAY: MOVING BEYOND POPULAR DISCOURSES

We have a lot of thinking to do when it comes to the future of digital play. More specifically, we desperately need to develop a possibility thinking mindset in relation to this issue. Possibility thinking is the shift from thinking about what is in front of us to thinking about the multiple 'what ifs' that surround us (Burnard et al., 2006; Cremin et al., 2006; Craft, 2015). So rather than seeing a plastic bottle of water, possibility thinking enables us to see its myriad potential uses, including as a vase, or a mini green house, or a container for storing beads or buttons, or as a weapon in a water fight and so on. In thinking about the future of digital play in early childhood, we desperately need to engage in possibility thinking. We need to delve into the 'what ifs' that surround digital play rather than thinking of digital play as a ready-made and unmodifiable package of activities that can only be integrated into particular contexts and used in particular ways.

In conversations with students and practitioners in early childhood, I am always struck by their sense that they need to live with what they see as the norms of digital play. For example, I have witnessed many experienced and trainee practitioners set up children's engagement with digital tablets as a solitary activity. They assume that children will not collaborate around tablets and that this kind of digital play is best suited to a single child engaging with the device, and the others waiting their turn. In fact, I have seen this not just in relation to digital tablets, but also in the case of the Interactive Whiteboard, despite its large size, which would be an ideal environment for collaborative creativity in many respects (Sakr and Scollan, 2019). Why do practitioners tend to assume that one device can only be used by one child at a time? We seem to have internalised messages from the popular media – both news and advertising – that suggest that digital devices belong to individuals, do not suit collaborative activities, and cannot facilitate social connection between those in the immediate surroundings. These messages have then filtered through into practice, and the norms are reinforced because it is the norms that have been planned for.

How can we start to question these portrayals of digital technologies in childhood, and more importantly, start to experiment with the alternatives? The starting point is surely to become more aware of the sorts of messages about digital technologies and digital play that we are constantly exposed to. In the previous chapter, we introduced the concept of discourses – systems of thinking and talking about a particular issue – and explored how they influence our practices. For example, if we are surrounded by a discourse that children's screen time needs to be limited, then being exposed to this way of thinking and talking will make us more likely to carry forward that message, without necessarily stopping to think about whether the construct of 'screen time' is actually a helpful way of thinking about the issue.

Let us consider a personal example. If I, as a mother, watch a news story about children spending too long on screens and parents treating digital technologies as 'babysitters' when they are tired or need to complete housework, then I am more likely to think of my own actions in these terms. To begin with, I am much more likely to count up the amount of screen time that my children 'consume' over the course of the day. I know that this seems like a simple move, but measuring the length of an activity has important implications for our engagement with the activity more generally. Beyond counting, I am likely to internalise the guilt that is part of this media message, and this will affect my behaviours in various ways. I might try to reduce my children's screen time and I might be careful not to leave the children alone with their devices so that I cannot be accused of using a digital babysitter, but I will probably also be less truthful with myself and with others about the amount of screen time that the children engage in because I worry that I will be judged. I will essentially start to regulate myself as a result of the exposure to the discourses surrounding the issues. In regulating myself, it becomes increasingly difficult to question the discourse that shaped the behaviours in the first place and close to impossible to think about alternative ways of thinking and doing digital play.

The first step is critical questioning: to be aware when reporters talk about 'screen time' on the news that this is indeed a discourse, that this is not 'the truth' but rather a version of particular truths packaged in particular ways. Through this awareness, I can start to see what is made possible and what is lost as a result of this particular discourse. For example, we might notice that when we think in terms of 'screen time', children are rendered as passive consumers of digital technologies, rather than active agents or cultural producers. Compare the term 'screen time' with the term 'digital engagement'. These terms create completely different impressions of children and childhood; one is passive and the other active. Beyond the limiting conceptualisation of children, the term 'screen time' focuses our attention on the beginning and end points of the activity rather than on the nature of the activity itself (Squire & Steinkuehler, 2017). From the perspective of early childhood education, this is a troubling development. Surely, as practitioners in early childhood, our focus should be on the quality of children's engagement, rather than on the boundaries in time according to which they transition between different activities. If we buy into the 'screen time' dosage model when thinking about digital play, we are at great risk of losing our sense of how a particular activity has meaning for a particular child in a particular context.

DEVELOPING A 'GUERRILLA DESIGN' APPROACH TO DIGITAL PLAY

As we become increasingly critical about the popular discourses that surround digital play, we can start to experiment with alternative forms of digital play that undo associations with digital play that cause us concern. To give an example, one prominent discourse is that in our digital world, life has become more manic, more fast-paced and children (and adults) are no longer able to concentrate on one thing at a time. But does digital play have to be fast-paced? Why do we see it as inevitable that digital play is fast-paced? Are there forms of digital play currently available for children that celebrate slowing down? If not, what would slowed-down digital play for children look like? What would it take to slow down digital play, or how could we playfully experiment with pace in the context of children's digital play?

Asking questions about the nature of digital play (e.g. 'Does digital play have to be X?', 'What if children's digital play involved more Y?') does not require technical or design expertise. In fact, as students and practitioners of early childhood we are in a better position than those from a computer science background to come up with exciting forms of digital play for early childhood. To some extent, we can even start to implement some of the new possibilities in children's digital play for ourselves. If we are curious and willing to explore – and crucially, if we can find the time in the context of our work and lives to carry out these explorations – we can find digital resources that are freely or cheaply available and use these to realise our envisaged digital play possibilities. I call this 'guerrilla design' – making use of whatever we can find in order to implement new possibilities in digital play. I am convinced that it is one of the most empowering processes that educators can go through in relation to children's digital engagement.

How might the 'guerrilla design' process look in action? In writing this book, for example, I have become interested in the potentials of digital play for enabling outdoor play and exploration and in how digital outdoor play might challenge the common discourse that posits digital play as a barrier to outdoor play and a love of nature. When researching digital play in outdoor environments, I did indeed come across lots of cutting-edge digital games designs that are specifically designed to get children moving about outside. However, many of these digital games are not readily available, and the evidence that surrounds their use suggests that they can be quite constraining in terms of children's playfulness and creativity (e.g. see Hitron et al., 2018). This might be because the games are actually a bit 'over-designed' as a result of their emergence within the digital games industry, rather than stemming from a love of being with young children. As early childhood practitioners, we know that the best play comes about in a free-flow context where children take the lead, improvise and have to be resourceful. This would suggest that what we need is not a technically impressive pre-packaged outdoor digital game, but rather some digital resources that facilitate children's spontaneous outdoor play and exploration.

What might this look like? Here are some initial thoughts, which I share just to give you a sense of what the first stages of guerrilla design would look like:

- A simple camera app might encourage creative outdoor exploration. In White (2015), the children's photographs of the natural environment were provocative and rich; the photography did not appear to get in the way of an intense engagement with the outdoor environment, but tuned the children into different aspects of the natural environment.
- What if there were some simple instructions to children, embedded in the camera app, that encouraged them to engage in more playful forms of photography? Simple audio instructions might be 'Look up, what's happening in the sky right now?', or 'Get down low and take a photo while you lie down', or 'Take a selfie with a bit of nature'.
- What if the camera had a really powerful zoom, so it was a bit like looking through a magnifying glass? What if other typical scientific apparatus were part of or attached to the phone/tablet, for instance a thermometer, or a litmus test probe for checking soil acidity. Some of these potentials were explored with older children in the Ambient Wood project (Rogers et al., 2002).
- What if the children could also record sounds that they hear, and combine these sounds from nature (and from other sources) to make an audio collage or a piece of music?

None of these ideas are at all revolutionary. In fact, all of these functions are available in apps that are cheap or free to download. Some of these ideas have been explored with children, though generally children in middle rather than early childhood. The fact that there is little that is genuinely new here is a fundamental aspect of guerrilla design. The point is not to come up with something so wonderfully original that the resources to make it a reality are not readily available. Instead, guerrilla design relies on thinking creatively about what digital play might involve (what you would like it to involve) and then finding out what resources are readily available in order to make something like this possible. You might use reflection exercises and research studies as a way of scaffolding these explorations and recording what happens at each stage, but ultimately guerrilla design is something that should feel fun and spontaneous. It is a form of adult play – where the commitment is to resourcefulness as a process rather than a particular outcome. Guerrilla design requires that we stop seeing ourselves as 'responders' to the digital play phenomenon and start believing in ourselves as adventurers and creators for the sake of the young children we work and live with.

WHAT CHILDREN NEED FROM US

The sections above suggest that creativity, curiosity and criticality are fundamental aspects of our approach to the future of digital play in early childhood. This is not just in order to facilitate our contribution to shaping digital play; it is essential because these are exactly the aspects of an approach that children themselves need to develop and apply to their engagement in digital play.

One aspect of the popular discourse that surrounds children's digital play is the idea that children first and foremost need our protection. The research of Willett (2015; see previous chapter for a summary of the research) demonstrated how parents were encouraged through popular discourses to think about themselves as 'good parents' when they kept their children safe in particular online spaces that were both socially and developmentally 'appropriate' for children, such as ClubPenguin or Poptropica. The 'good parents' were those who deposited their children into a safe corner of what was seen to be a dangerous and scary online world. Intensely commercial child-friendly sites acted much like a playpen; a child-proofed corner among the hazards of the living room. Let us take this metaphor further though, to think about the impact of this discourse on children's experiences of the world. We would struggle with the idea of keeping a child in a playpen for prolonged periods, since we would think that the exploration of the potentially unsafe space is critical for them. They need to have richer experiences than what the playpen can offer and they need to learn about how to cope with the hazards they encounter through their instinctive exploration. The world of digital play is similar: the playpens of highly commercialised online virtual worlds might be helpful for ensuring that children are safe at particular points in time, but children also need – for their learning and wellbeing – to explore, roam and encounter dangers that they learn to navigate and manage. To cope with the hazards and make the most of this exploration, children need creativity, curiosity and criticality: the 3Cs.

Adults are central in helping children to develop the 3Cs in their digital play. They can do this through modelling, questioning and creating activities that encourage children to develop these characteristics. Probably the most impactful contribution adults can make here is through co-playing, since co-playing creates a context in which all of these other forms of scaffolding can occur. The benefits of co-playing have been deeply underestimated. Craft et al. (2012) discuss the power of 'meddling in the middle' through co-playing with children, and this applies to digital play equally. Co-playing not only creates a context for scaffolding behaviours, but also deepens our sense of shared experience and how much we enjoy the company of one another.

In order to engage in co-playing, we need to have a genuine interest in and curiosity about digital play. It might seem like quite an unorthodox suggestion, but the most helpful thing we can do as practitioners and parents is perhaps to develop our own digital play habits and be experimental in the forms of digital play that we engage with as part of our everyday leisure.

I recently ran a workshop for early childhood practitioners, designed to get them engaging in a hands-on way with a wide range of apps designed for very young children. I was taken aback by the tendency of the practitioners to go straight to the 'instructions' or 'rationale' for the app – a screen of dense text that they could read and summarise – rather than wanting to learn about the app through getting 'stuck in' with what the app had to offer experientially. The practitioners' first priority was often to look for a verbal articulation of the educational potential of the app, rather than approach the app as the children in their care might do: with intrigue, with a desire to engage actively, and with enjoyment and meaning-making in the moment rather than abstract notions of 'educational potential'. While we all recognise the pressures on early childhood settings when it comes to intentional planning, digital play requires us to adopt a more exploratory approach and to learn through experience. We want this for the children we support, so we need to apply this attitude in our own approach.

SO WHAT NEXT?

There is no doubt that we need more research that focuses on digital play in early childhood. Only a small proportion of the research investigating digital engagement focuses on young children – in fact the younger the children, the fewer the research studies that help us to make sense of digital play. Although my own research stems from a critical paradigm, and utilises observations as the primary research method, I recognise that there is a need for research from all different research traditions and methodological frameworks. We need more psychological research on children's attentional distribution during digital play, and this might be conducted through experiments in laboratory conditions. Simultaneously, we need more sociological research that reports on observations within naturalistic settings, unpicking the complex social trends that are shaping children's contemporary experiences of play. As early childhood practitioners, we are likely to have a particular skill for 'observation' since this is a fundamental aspect of practice in the sector. Through your own close observations of digital play as it unfolds, you will be able to zoom in and out, to see the minute details of the child(ren)'s unfolding interactions in digital play, but also to become more aware of the complexities at work, not least the messiness of the term 'digital play' and the manifold connections and flows that make up even the smallest moment of digital play in context.

Within and beyond research, we need to develop our own digital play practices in order to build the 3Cs – criticality, creativity and curiosity – and help children to develop their own empowering approach to digital play and their digital engagement more generally. We develop criticality through unpicking the popular discourses that surround digital play and inevitably influence our everyday behaviours. We develop creativity through possibility thinking around digital play – questioning the existing discourses around digital play, visualising alternative discourses, but also visualising new forms of digital play that challenge our existing conceptions of what digital play actually is. We develop curiosity through being prepared to explore digital play for ourselves in a hands-on way, prioritising enjoyment and engagement over 'educational potential' abstractly articulated. Curiosity is key in finding cheaply or freely available resources that we can use as part of the guerrilla design process of creating new forms of digital play that are most resonant for the children we live and work with in everyday life.

REFERENCES

Abidin, C. (2017). #familygoals: Family influencers, calibrated amateurism, and justifying young digital labor. *Social Media + Society*, *3*(2). Available at: https://journals.sagepub.com/doi/abs/10.1177/2056305117707191 (accessed 29 April 2019).

Abric, J.C. (1971). Experimental study of group creativity: Task representation, group structure, and performance. *European Journal of Social Psychology*, *1*(3), 311–326.

Arvidsson, A., Caliandro, A., Airoldi, M., & Barina, S. (2016). Crowds and value: Italian directioners on Twitter. *Information, Communication & Society*, *19*, 921–939.

Barad, K. (2007). *Meeting the universe halfway: Quantum physics and the entanglement of matter and meaning*. Durham, NC: Duke University Press.

Bassiouni, D.H., & Hackley, C. (2016). Video games and young children's evolving sense of identity: A qualitative study. *Young Consumers*, *17*(2), 127–142.

Beyens, I., & Beullens, K. (2017). Parent–child conflict about children's tablet use: The role of parental mediation. *New Media & Society*, *19*(12), 2075–2093.

Bezemer, J., & Kress, G. (2015). *Multimodality, learning and communication: A social semiotic frame*. London: Routledge.

Bianchi-Berthouze, N., Kim, W.W., & Patel, D. (2007). Does body movement engage you more in digital game play? And why? In *International Conference on Affective Computing and Intelligent Interaction* (pp. 102–113). Berlin, Heidelberg: Springer.

Björkvall, A. (2014). Practices of visual communication in a primary school classroom: Digital image collection as a potential semiotic mode. *Classroom Discourse*, *5*(1), 22–37.

Björkvall, A., & Engblom, C. (2010). Young children's exploration of semiotic resources during unofficial computer activities in the classroom. *Journal of Early Childhood Literacy, 10*(3), 271–293.

Bohanek, J.G., Marin, K A., Fivush, R., & Duke, M.P. (2006). Family narrative interaction and children's sense of self. *Family Process, 45*(1), 39–54.

Bosacki, S.L., Varnish, A., & Akseer, S. (2008). Children's gendered sense of self and play as represented through drawings and written descriptions. *Canadian Journal of School Psychology, 23*(2), 190–205.

Boulos, M.N.K., & Yang, S.P. (2013). Exergames for health and fitness: The roles of GPS and geosocial apps. *International Journal of Health Geographics, 12*(18), 1–7.

Bragg, S., Buckingham, D., Russell, R., & Willett, R. (2011). Too much, too soon? Children, 'sexualization' and consumer culture. *Sex Education, 11*(3), 279–292.

Brasel, S.A., & Gips, J. (2011). Media multitasking behavior: Concurrent television and computer usage. *Cyberpsychology, Behavior, and Social Networking, 14*(9), 527–534.

Brockman, R., Jago, R., & Fox, K. R. (2011). Children's active play: Self-reported motivators, barriers and facilitators. *BMC Public Health, 11*(1), 461.

Bruce, B.C. (1997). Critical issues literacy technologies: What stance should we take? *Journal of Literacy Research, 29*(2), 289–309.

Bruce, T. (1991). *Time to play in early childhood education.* London: Edward Arnold, Hodder & Stoughton.

Bruce, T. (2012). *Learning through play, for babies, toddlers and young children.* London: Hachette UK.

Bruner, J., Lucariello, J., & Nelson, K. (1989). *Narratives from the crib.* Cambridge, MA: Harvard University Press.

Buckingham, D. (2007). Selling childhood? Children and consumer culture. *Journal of Children and Media, 1*(1), 15–24.

Buckingham, D., & de Block, L. (2007). *Global children, global media: Migration, media and childhood.* Basingstoke: Palgrave Macmillan.

Burnard, P., & Younker, B.A. (2008). Investigating children's musical interactions within the activities systems of group composing and arranging: An application of Engeström's activity theory. *International Journal of Educational Research, 47*(1), 60–74.

Burnard, P., Craft, A., Cremin, T., Duffy, B., Hanson, R., Keene, J., Haynes, L., & Burns, D. (2006). Documenting 'possibility thinking': A journey of collaborative enquiry. *International Journal of Early Years Education, 14*(3), 243–262.

Burnett, C. (2014). Investigating pupils' interactions around digital texts: A spatial perspective on the 'classroom-ness' of digital literacy practices in schools. *Educational Review, 66*(2), 192–209.

Burnett, C., & Merchant, G. (2018). Affective encounters: Enchantment and the possibility of reading for pleasure. *Literacy, 52*(2), 62–69.

Burnett, C., Merchant, G., Pahl, K., & Rowsell, J. (2014). The (im)materiality of literacy: The significance of subjectivity to new literacies research. *Discourse: Studies in the Cultural Politics of Education, 35*(1), 90–103.

Burnett, C., Merchant, G., Simpson, A., & Walsh, M. (2018). *The case of the iPad: Mobile literacies in education.* Singapore: Springer.

Cameron, D. (2001). *Working with spoken discourse.* London: Sage.

Canning, N., Payler, J., Horsley, K., & Gomez, C. (2017). An innovative methodology for capturing young children's curiosity, imagination and voices using a free app: Our story. *International Journal of Early Years Education, 25*(3), 292–307.

Carr, N. (2011). *The shallows: What the Internet is doing to our brains.* New York: WW Norton.

Carrier, L.M., Rosen, L.D., Cheever, N.A., & Lim, A.F. (2015). Causes, effects, and practicalities of everyday multitasking. *Developmental Review, 35,* 64–78.

Carrington, D. (2016). 'Three-quarters of UK children spend less time outdoors than prison inmates – survey', *The Guardian*, 25 March 2016. Available online at: https://www.theguardian.com/environment/2016/mar/25/three-quarters-of-uk-children-spend-less-time-outdoors-than-prison-inmates-survey

Chappell, K., Craft, A., Burnard, P., & Cremin, T. (2008). Question-posing and question-responding: The heart of 'Possibility Thinking' in the early years. *Early Years, 28*(3), 267–286.

Clements, R. (2004). An investigation of the status of outdoor play. *Contemporary Issues in Early Childhood, 5*(1), 68–80.

Cole, M., & Engeström, Y. (1993). A cultural–historical approach to distributed cognition. In G. Salomon (Ed.), *Distributed cognitions: Psychological and educational considerations* (pp. 1–46). Cambridge: Cambridge University Press.

Craft, A. (2012). Childhood in a digital age: Creative challenges for educational futures. *London Review of Education, 10*(2), 173–190.

Craft, A. (2013). Childhood, possibility thinking and wise, humanising educational futures. *International Journal of Educational Research, 61,* 126–134.

Craft, A. (2015). Possibility thinking: From what is to what might be. In R. Wegerif, L. Li, & J. C. Kaufman (Eds.), *The Routledge international handbook of research on teaching thinking* (pp. 177–191). London: Routledge.

Craft, A., McConnon, L., & Matthews, A. (2012). Child-initiated play and professional creativity: Enabling four-year-olds' possibility thinking. *Thinking Skills and Creativity, 7*(1), 48–61.

Craig, D., & Cunningham, S. (2017). Toy unboxing: Living in a(n unregulated) material world. *Media International Australia, 163*(1), 77–86.

Cremin, T., Burnard, P., & Craft, A. (2006). Pedagogy and possibility thinking in the early years. *Thinking Skills and Creativity, 1*(2), 108–119.

Crescenzi, L., Price, S., & Jewitt, C. (2014). Paint on the finger or paint on the screen: A comparative study. *Procedia – Social and Behavioral Sciences, 140*, 376–380.

Davies, D., Jindal-Snape, D., Collier, C., Digby, R., Hay, P., & Howe, A. (2013). Creative learning environments in education: A systematic literature review. *Thinking Skills and Creativity, 8*, 80–91.

Denmead, T., & Hickman, R. (2012). Viscerality and slowliness: An anatomy of artists' pedagogies of material and time. *International Journal of Education & the Arts, 13*(9). Available at: http://www.ijea.org/v13n9/

Dezuanni, M., & Knight, L. (2015). Networking iPads into preschool spaces. In M. Dezuanni, K. Dooley, S. Gattenhof, & L. Knight (Eds.), *iPads in the early years: Developing literacy and creativity* (pp. 142–161). London: Routledge.

Dodge, T., Barab, S., Stuckey, B., Warren, S., Heiselt, C., & Stein, R. (2008). Children's sense of self: Learning and meaning in the digital age. *Journal of Interactive Learning Research, 19*(2), 225–249.

Druga, S., Williams, R., Breazeal, C., & Resnick, M. (2017). Hey Google is it OK if I eat you?: Initial explorations in child–agent interaction. In *Proceedings of the 2017 Conference on Interaction Design and Children* (pp. 595–600). ACM.

Duerager, A., & Livingstone, S. (2012). *How can parents support children's internet safety?* London: EU Kids Online.

Duncum, P. (1999). A multiple pathways/multiple endpoints model of graphic development. *Visual Arts Research, 25*(2), 38–47.

Duncum, P. (2010). Seven principles for visual culture education. *Art Education, 63*(1), 6–10.

Duncum, P. (2019). Holly Banister: A social incentive account of exceptional drawing ability. In J. Osgood & M. Sakr (Eds.), *Postdevelopmental approaches to childhood art* (pp. 67–87). London: Bloomsbury.

Edwards, S. (2013). Digital play in the early years: A contextual response to the problem of integrating technologies and play-based pedagogies in the early childhood curriculum. *European Early Childhood Education Research Journal, 21*(2), 199–212.

Edwards, S. (2016). New concepts of play and the problem of technology, digital media and popular-culture integration with play-based learning in early childhood education. *Technology, Pedagogy and Education, 25*(4), 513–532.

Fiedler, F.E. (1962). Leader attitudes, group climate, and group creativity. *The Journal of Abnormal and Social Psychology, 65*(5), 308–318.

Fisher, M., Goddu, M.K., & Keil, F.C. (2015). Searching for explanations: How the Internet inflates estimates of internal knowledge. *Journal of Experimental Psychology: General, 144*(3), 674.

Flewitt, R., Kucirkova, N., & Messer, D. (2014). Touching the virtual, touching the real: iPads and enabling literacy for students experiencing disability. *Australian Journal of Language & Literacy, 37*(2), 107–116.

Gibson, J.J. (1961). Ecological optics. *Vision Research, 1*, 253–262.

Giddings, S. (2014). *Gameworlds: Virtual media and children's everyday play*. London: Bloomsbury.

Gillen, J., & Kucirkova, N. (2018). Percolating spaces: Creative ways of using digital technologies to connect young children's school and home lives. *British Journal of Educational Technology*, *49*(5), 834–846.

Glăveanu, V.P. (2010). Paradigms in the study of creativity: Introducing the perspective of cultural psychology. *New Ideas in Psychology*, *28*(1), 79–93.

Glăveanu, V.P. (2017). *Thinking through creativity and culture: Toward an integrated model*. London: Routledge.

Goffman, E. (1959). *The presentation of self in everyday life*. Edinburgh: University of Edinburgh Social Sciences Research Centre.

Goodwin, C. (2007). Participation, stance and affect in the organization of activities. *Discourse & Society*, *18*(1), 53–73.

Goodwin, M.H. (2006). Participation, affect, and trajectory in family directive/response sequences. *Text & Talk – An Interdisciplinary Journal of Language, Discourse Communication Studies*, *26*(4–5), 515–543.

Gray, P. (2011). The decline of play and the rise of psychopathology in children and adolescents. *American Journal of Play*, *3*(4), 443–463.

Greenfield, S. (2014). *Mind change: How digital technologies are leaving their mark on our brains*. London: Random House.

Greenfield, S. (2015). Susan Greenfield replies to Vaughan Bell and colleagues. *BMJ*, *351*, h4960.

Gronn, D., Scott, A., Edwards, S., & Henderson, M. (2014). 'Technological me': Young children's use of technology across their home and school contexts. *Technology, Pedagogy and Education*, *23*(4), 439–454.

Grossen, M. (2008). Methods for studying collaborative creativity: An original and adventurous blend. *Thinking Skills and Creativity*, *3*(3), 246–249.

Hämäläinen, R., & Vähäsantanen, K. (2011). Theoretical and pedagogical perspectives on orchestrating creativity and collaborative learning. *Educational Research Review*, *6*(3), 169–184.

Hayles, N.K. (2007). Hyper and deep attention: The generational divide in cognitive modes. *Profession*, *1*, 187–199.

Hefner, D., Knop, K., Schmitt, S., & Vorderer, P. (2019). Rules? Role model? Relationship? The impact of parents on their children's problematic mobile phone involvement. *Media Psychology*, *22*(1), 82–108.

Henkel, L.A. (2014). Point-and-shoot memories: The influence of taking photos on memory for a museum tour. *Psychological Science*, *25*(2), 396–402.

Herrington, S., & Brussoni, M. (2015). Beyond physical activity: The importance of play and nature-based play spaces for children's health and development. *Current Obesity Reports*, *4*(4), 477–483.

Hess, A. (2015). The selfie assemblage. *International Journal of Communication, 9*(18), 1629–1646. Available at: https://ijoc.org/index.php/ijoc/article/viewFile/3147/1389 (accessed 07.08.19)

Hitron, T., David, I., Ofer, N., Grishko, A., Wald, I.Y., Erel, H., & Zuckerman, O. (2018). Digital outdoor play: Benefits and risks from an interaction design perspective. In *Proceedings of the 2018 CHI Conference on Human Factors in Computing Systems* (p. 284). ACM Digital Library.

Hughes, B. (2002). *A playworker's taxonomy of play types* (2nd ed.). London: PlayLink.

Hughes, B. (2011). *Evolutionary playwork* (2nd ed.). London: Routledge.

Karageorgiadis, E. (2016). Interview with Instituto Alana, São Paulo, 14 July.

Kelly, C. (2015). 'Let's do some jumping together': Intergenerational participation in the use of remote technology to co-construct social relations over distance. *Journal of Early Childhood Research, 13*(1), 29–46.

Kincheloe, J. (2011). Home alone and bad to the bone: The advent of a postmodern childhood. In S.R. Steinberg (Ed.), *Kinderculture: The corporate construction of childhood* (pp. 438–480). Boulder, CO: Westview Press.

Kirschner, P.A., & De Bruyckere, P. (2017). The myths of the digital native and the multitasker. *Teaching and Teacher Education, 67*, 135–142.

Kollmeyer, B. (2015). Ready to be hypnotized by 'toddler crack'?, *MediaWatch.com*. Available at: www.marketwatch.com/story/ready-to-get-hypnotized-by-toddler-crack-2015-04-07 (accessed 29 July 2016).

Kress, G. (2005a). *Before writing: Rethinking the paths to literacy*. London: Routledge.

Kress, G. (2005b). Gains and losses: New forms of texts, knowledge, and learning. *Computers and Composition, 22*(1), 5–22.

Kucirkova, N., & Sakr, M. (2015). Child–father creative text-making at home with crayons, iPad collage & PC. *Thinking Skills and Creativity, 17*, 59–73.

Kucirkova, N., Messer, D., & Sheehy, K. (2014). The effects of personalisation on young children's spontaneous speech during shared book reading. *Journal of Pragmatics, 71*, 45–55.

Kucirkova, N., Messer, D., Sheehy, K., & Flewitt, R. (2013). Sharing personalised stories on iPads: A close look at one parent–child interaction. *Literacy, 47*(3), 115–122.

Lamb, B. (2007). Dr. Mashup or, why educators should learn to stop worrying and love the remix. *Educause Review, 42*(4), 13–14.

Lankshear, C., & Knobel, M. (2006). *New literacies: Everyday practices and classroom learning*. Milton Keynes: Open University Press.

Lastowka, G. (2012). Minecraft, intellectual property, and the future of copyright, *Gamasutra*. Available at: www.gamasutra.com/view/feature/134958/minecraft_intellectual_property_.php (accessed 29 April 2009).

Livingstone, S., Mascheroni, G., Dreier, M., Chaudron, S., & Lagae, K. (2015). *How parents of young children manage digital devices at home: The role of income, education and parental style*. London: London School of Economics.

Loh, K.K., & Kanai, R. (2016). How has the Internet reshaped human cognition? *The Neuroscientist, 22*(5), 506–520.

Magnusson, L.O. (2018). Photographic agency and agency of photographs: Three-year-olds and digital cameras. *Australasian Journal of Early Childhood, 43*(3), 34.

Mangen, A. (2010). Point and click: Theoretical and phenomenological reflections on the digitization of early childhood education. *Contemporary Issues in Early Childhood, 11*(4), 415–431.

Marsh, J. (2016). 'Unboxing' videos: Co-construction of the child as cyberflâneur. *Discourse: Studies in the Cultural Politics of Education, 37*(3), 369–380.

Marsh, J.A. (2017). The internet of toys: A posthuman and multimodal analysis of connected play. *Teachers College Record, 119*(15). Available at: http://eprints.whiterose.ac.uk/113557/ (accessed 07.08.2019)

Marsh, J., & Bishop, J. (2012). Rewind and replay? Television and play in the 1950s/1960s and 2010s. *International Journal of Play, 1*(3), 279–291.

Marsh, J., Hannon, P., Lewis, M., & Ritchie, L. (2017). Young children's initiation into family literacy practices in the digital age. *Journal of Early Childhood Research, 15*(1), 47–60.

Marsh, J., Plowman, L., Yamada-Rice, D., Bishop, J., & Scott, F. (2016). Digital play: A new classification. *Early Years, 36*(3), 242–253.

Martínez, C., & Olsson, T. (2018). Making sense of YouTubers: How Swedish children construct and negotiate the YouTuber Misslisibell as a girl celebrity. *Journal of Children and Media, 13*(1), 1–17.

Marwick, A.E., & boyd, d. (2011a). I tweet honestly, I tweet passionately: Twitter users, context collapse, and the imagined audience. *New Media & Society, 13*(1), 114–133.

Marwick, A., & boyd, d. (2011b). To see and be seen: Celebrity practice on Twitter. *Convergence, 17*(2), 139–158.

Mavers, D. (2007). Semiotic resourcefulness: A young child's email exchange as design. *Journal of Early Childhood Literacy, 7*(2), 155–176.

Mavoa, J., Gibbs, M., & Carter, M. (2017). Constructing the young child media user in Australia: A discourse analysis of Facebook comments. *Journal of Children and Media, 11*(3), 330–346.

McLennan, D.M.P. (2010). Process or product? The argument for aesthetic exploration in the early years. *Early Childhood Education Journal, 38*(2), 81–85.

Nansen, B., & Jayemanne, D. (2016). Infants, interfaces, and intermediation: Digital parenting and the production of 'iPad Baby' videos on YouTube. *Journal of Broadcasting & Electronic Media, 60*(4), 587–603.

Nathanson, A.I. (2002). The unintended effects of parental mediation of television on adolescents. *Media Psychology, 4*(3), 207–230.

Nelson, M.E., Hull, G.A., & Roche-Smith, J. (2008). Challenges of multimedia self-presentation: Taking, and mistaking, the show on the road. *Written Communication, 25*(4), 415–440.

O'Brien, J., & Smith, J. (2002). Childhood transformed? Risk perceptions and the decline of free play. *British Journal of Occupational Therapy, 65*(3), 123–128.

Palmer, S. (2015). *Toxic childhood: How the modern world is damaging our children and what we can do about it* (2nd ed.). London: Orion Publishing.

Park, C.S., & Kaye, B.K. (2018). Smartphone and self-extension: Functionally, anthropomorphically, and ontologically extending self via the smartphone. *Mobile Media & Communication 7*(2): 215–231. Available at: https://journals.sagepub.com/doi/abs/10.1177/2050157918808327 (accessed 07.08.19).

Paulus, P.B., & Nijstad, B.A. (Eds.) (2003). *Group creativity: Innovation through collaboration*. Oxford: Oxford University Press.

Pedersen, I., & Aspevig, K. (2018). Being Jacob: Young children, automedial subjectivity, and child social media influencers. *M/C Journal, 21*(2). Available at: http://www.journal.media-culture.org.au/index.php/mcjournal/article/view/1352

Plowman, L., & Stephen, C. (2005). Children, play, and computers in pre-school education. *British Journal of Educational Technology, 36*(2), 145–157.

Plowman, L., Stephen, C., & McPake, J. (2010). Supporting young children's learning with technology at home and in preschool. *Research Papers in Education, 25*(1), 93–113.

Prensky, M. (2001). Digital natives, digital immigrants part 1. *On the Horizon, 9*(5), 1–6.

Price, S., & Rogers, Y. (2004). Let's get physical: The learning benefits of interacting in digitally augmented physical spaces. *Computers & Education, 43*(1–2), 137–151.

Ra, C.K., Cho, J., Stone, M.D., De La Cerda, J., Goldenson, N.I., Moroney, E., Tung, I., Lee, S.S., & Leventhal, A.M. (2018). Association of digital media use with subsequent symptoms of attention-deficit/hyperactivity disorder among adolescents. *JAMA, 320*(3), 255–263.

Robinson, K. (2010). Changing education paradigms. *TED Talk*. Available at: www.ted.com/talks/ken_robinson_changing_education_paradigms (accessed 29 January 2019).

Rogers, Y., Scaife, M., Gabrielli, S., Smith, H., & Harris, E. (2002). A conceptual framework for mixed reality environments: Designing novel learning activities for young children. *Presence, 11*(6), 677–686.

Rojas-Drummond, S.M., Albarrán, C.D., & Littleton, K. (2008). Collaboration, creativity and the co-construction of oral and written texts. *Thinking Skills and Creativity, 3*(3), 177–191.

Rose, S., & Whitty, P. (2010). 'Where do we find the time to do this?' Struggling against the tyranny of time. *Alberta Journal of Educational Research, 56*(3), 257–273.

Sakr, M. (2017). *Digital technologies in early childhood art: Enabling playful experiences*. London: Bloomsbury.

Sakr, M., & Kucirkova, N. (2017). Parent–child moments of meeting in art-making with collage, iPad, Tuxpaint and crayons. *International Journal of Education & the Arts, 18*(2). Available at: http://www.ijea.org/v18n2/ (accessed 07.08.19)

Sakr, M. & Scollan, A. (2019). The screen and the sand-timer: The integration of the interactive whiteboard into an early years free-flow learning environment. *Journal of Early Childhood Research*. Available at: https://doi.org/10.1177/1476718X19851538

Sakr, M., Connelly, V., & Wild, M. (2016). 'Evil Cats' and 'Jelly Floods': Young children's collective constructions of digital art making in the early years classroom. *Journal of Research in Childhood Education, 30*(1), 128–141.

Sakr, M., Connelly, V., & Wild, M. (2018). Imitative or iconoclastic? How young children use ready-made images in digital art. *International Journal of Art & Design Education, 37*(1), 41–52.

Salvucci, D.D., & Taatgen, N.A. (2008). Threaded cognition: An integrated theory of concurrent multitasking. *Psychological Review, 115*(1), 101.

Sawyer, R.K. (2004). Creative teaching: Collaborative discussion as disciplined improvisation. *Educational Researcher, 33*(2), 12–20.

Sawyer, R.K. (Ed.) (2011). *Structure and improvisation in creative teaching*. Cambridge: Cambridge University Press.

Schilhab, T. (2017). Impact of iPads on break-time in primary schools – a Danish context. *Oxford Review of Education, 43*(3), 261–275.

Seitinger, S. (2006). An ecological approach to children's playground props. In *Proceedings of the 2006 Conference on Interaction Design and Children* (pp. 117–120). ACM.

Selwyn, N. (2009). The digital native – myth and reality. *Aslib Proceedings, 61*(4), 364–379.

Senft, T.M. (2008). *Camgirls: Celebrity & community in the age of social networks*. New York: Peter Lang.

Siau, K.L. (1995). Group creativity and technology. *The Journal of Creative Behavior, 29*(3), 201–216.

Skår, M., & Krogh, E. (2009). Changes in children's nature-based experiences near home: From spontaneous play to adult-controlled, planned and organised activities. *Children's Geographies, 7*(3), 339–354.

Soler-Adillon, J., & Parés, N. (2009). Interactive slide: An interactive playground to promote physical activity and socialization of children. In *CHI '09 Extended Abstracts on Human Factors in Computing Systems* (pp. 2407–2416). ACM.

Soute, I., Markopoulos, P., & Magielse, R. (2010). Head Up Games: Combining the best of both worlds by merging traditional and digital play. *Personal and Ubiquitous Computing, 14*(5), 435–444.

Squire, K., & Steinkuehler, C. (2017). The problem with screen time. *Teachers College Record, 119*(12), 1–24.

Steinberg, S.R. (2011). *Kinderculture: The corporate construction of childhood*. Boulder, CO: Westview Press.

Steiner-Adair, C., & Barker, T.H. (2013). *The big disconnect: Protecting childhood and family relationships in the digital age*. New York: Harper Business.

Stern, D.N. (2000). *Interpersonal world of the infant: A view from psychoanalysis and development psychology*. London: Basic books.

Stern, D.N. (2004). *The present moment in psychotherapy and everyday life* (Norton series on interpersonal neurobiology). London: WW Norton & Company.

Stiegler, B. (1998). *Technics and time: The fault of Epimetheus* (Vol. 1). Stanford, CA: Stanford University Press.

Strong-Wilson, T., & Ellis, J. (2007). Children and place: Reggio Emilia's environment as third teacher. *Theory into Practice, 46*(1), 40–47.

Sutton-Smith, B. (2001). *The ambiguity of play*. Cambridge, MA : Harvard University Press.

Szyba, C.M. (1999). Why do some teachers resist offering appropriate, open-ended art activities for young children? *Young Children, 54*(1), 16–20.

Tandon, P.S., Zhou, C., & Christakis, D.A. (2012). Frequency of parent-supervised outdoor play of US preschool-aged children. *Archives of Pediatrics & Adolescent Medicine, 166*(8), 707–712.

Tarr, P. (2004). Consider the walls. *Young Children, 59*(3), 88–92.

Thibault, M. (2016). Post-digital games. The influence of nostalgia in indie games' graphic regimes. *GAMEVIRONMENTS, 4*, 1–23.

Thompson, C.M. (2003). Kinderculture in the art classroom: Early childhood art and the mediation of culture. *Studies in Art Education, 44*(2), 135–146.

Trafi-Prats, L. (2019). Thinking childhood art with care in an ecology of practices. In J. Osgood & M. Sakr (Eds.), *Postdevelopmental approaches to childhood art*. London: Bloomsbury. pp.191–210.

Turkle, S. (2017). *Alone together: Why we expect more from technology and less from each other*. London: Hachette UK.

Vass, E. (2007). Exploring processes of collaborative creativity – The role of emotions in children's joint creative writing. *Thinking Skills and Creativity, 2*(2), 107–117.

Veitch, J., Bagley, S., Ball, K., & Salmon, J. (2006). Where do children usually play? A qualitative study of parents' perceptions of influences on children's active free-play. *Health & Place, 12*(4), 383–393.

White, E.J. (2015). Seeing is believing? Insights from young children in nature. *International Journal of Early Childhood, 47*(1), 171–188.

Willett, R.J. (2015). The discursive construction of 'good parenting' and digital media – the case of children's virtual world games. *Media, Culture & Society, 37*(7), 1060–1075.

Wilson, B., & Wilson, M. (1977). An iconoclastic view of the imagery sources in the drawings of young people. *Art Education, 30*(1), 4–11.

Wilson, D. (2011). Brutally unfair tactics totally ok now: On self-effacing games and unachievements. *Game Studies, 11*(1). Available at: http://gamestudies.org/1101/articles/Wilson

Wilson, J. (2005). Indie rocks! Mapping independent video game design. *Media International Australia incorporating Culture and Policy, 115*(1), 109–122.

Witten, K., Kearns, R., Carroll, P., Asiasiga, L., & Tava'e, N. (2013). New Zealand parents' understandings of the intergenerational decline in children's independent outdoor play and active travel. *Children's Geographies, 11*(2), 215–229.

Wohlwend, K.E. (2013). *Literacy playshop: New literacies, popular media, and play in the early childhood classroom.* New York: Teachers College Press.

Wohlwend, K.E. (2015). One screen, many fingers: Young children's collaborative literacy play with digital puppetry apps and touchscreen technologies. *Theory Into Practice, 54*(2), 154–162.

Wohlwend, K. (2017a). Chasing literacies across action texts and augmented realities: E-books, animated apps, and Pokémon go. In C. Burnett, G. Merchant, A. Simpson, & M. Walsh (Eds.), *The case of the iPad* (pp. 49–66). Singapore: Springer.

Wohlwend, K.E. (2017b). Who gets to play? Access, popular media and participatory literacies. *Early Years, 37*(1), 62–76.

Wooldridge, M.B., & Shapka, J. (2012). Playing with technology: Mother–toddler interaction scores lower during play with electronic toys. *Journal of Applied Developmental Psychology, 33*(5), 211–218.

Zhao, S., & Zappavigna, M. (2018). 13 digital scrapbooks, everyday aesthetics, and the curatorial self. In E.S. Tonnessen & F. Forsgren (Eds.), *Multimodality and aesthetics* (pp. 218–235). London: Routledge.

INDEX

3Cs of digital play 148

active digital play 35–8
active mediation 91, 94
ADHD (attention deficit hyperactivity disorder) 109
   and fast-paced digital play 103–6
   research 104–5
advertising 88, 90
affective alignment 25–6, 31
   case study 27
affinity groups 113, 122
affordances 14–15, 20, 21, 31
Alexa 27, 28, 76–7
   case study 88
Ambient Wood project 36–7
'angry birds' (video game) 98
anthropomorphic extended self 121
apps (smartphone applications)
   Kids Doodle 39, 70
   Mr Glue 112
   Our Story 123
   outdoor play and exploration 58–9
   Puppet Pals 21–2
   research 78–9
   Sarah and Duck case study 1
   Spotify 84
   Squiggle 39, 67
   story-making 113
   Toca Nature 102
art-making 40, 71–2
attention 97–8
   allocation in digital play environments 98–100
   case studies 98, 102
   distractibility 99
   fast-paced digital play and ADHD 103–6
   independent games industry 106–8
   rapid shifting of 98
   research as problematic 97–8
   scattered 100–2
augmented landscapes and playgrounds 37
automedial subjectivity 86–7

Baby Shark (music video) 85
Bassiouni, D.H. & Hackley, C. 114
Björkvall, A. 75–6
block areas 59
Brasel, S.A. & Gips, J. 101
broken games 107–8
Brutally Unfair Tactics Totally Ok Now (BUTTON) (game) 107–8
bullying 52

calibrated amateurism 116
child social media influencers 86–7
childhood
   commercialisation of 88–91, 94
   influence of social trends 141
children
   as consumers 90
   needs of 55, 147–9
   time spent on digital screens 54, 92–3, 129, 130, 131, 144, 145
children's digital engagement 145
   commercial purposes 131
   perceived as a loss 131
children's literacy 21, 22
choosing time 13
classroom-ness 16
ClubPenguin 131
co-playing 70, 132, 148
co-use 92, 94
cognition 55
cognitive processing 98–9

cognitive shifts 99, 108
collaboration 16
  lack of 14, 15
collaborative creativity 19–22, 31
  case study 23–4, 39
  we-paradigm of 19
collecting digital images 75–6
commercialisation of childhood 88–91, 94
communication, open and active 92
computers, interaction with other digital devices 99, 101
connected play 44, 134, 143
  research 45–6
connectedness vs. connection 28–30, 32
  research 29–30
context of digital play 125–6
  blurring the boundaries 134–6
  case study 126
  challenging popular discourses 130–4
  discourses 131, 132, 137
  intermediation 127, 137
  mediation 126–30, 137
  reactive supervision 126, 137
conversational agents (CAs) 77
cooperative play 19
copying 74, 75
creativity 3, 40
  ready-made materials 74, 80, 81
  see also collaborative creativity; imagination
Cremin et al. 69–70
cultural investment 15
cultural products 84–5

diffractive analysis 116–17
digital cameras 116–17
digital craft 106, 109
digital disconnect 132–3, 134
digital engagement of children see children's digital engagement
digital environments
  boundaries and rules 78
  connection with physical environments 44–5
  creative play 73–4
  ready-made materials 73–4, 80
digital footprint 129–30
digital image collection 75–6
digital images 75–6
digital kinderculture 94
digital media 84–5, 135
digital natives 127–8
digital photography 37–8
digital play
  blurring the boundaries 134–6
  challenging popular discourses 130–4
  children's future lives 86–7
  creativity and art-making 40

  fast-paced 103–6, 146
  guerilla design approach 140, 145–7
  intangibility of 39
  media representation of 129–30
  mediating 126–30, 137
  multi-dimensional nature of 142–3
  negative issues surrounding 2, 3, 51–2
  observing 1–2, 4
  possibility thinking 144–5
  props 56–7
  shaping the future of 140–50
  slowing down 106–8
  social trends influencing childhood 141
  working definition 135
  see also context of digital play
digital remix 74, 75
digital scrapbooks 118
digital visual media 87
disability, iPads and touch 41–2
discourses 131, 132, 137, 141
distal guided interaction 17
distributed cognition 55
drawing
  on an iPad 40, 41, 41–2
  with a pencil 41

Edwards, S. 16
ethical issues 8–9
evolution 55
executive control 99
extended self 120, 121
external transactive memory 99

Facetime 28, 32
family influencers 117
fast-paced digital play 103–6, 106, 146
finger painting 40
fire, making of 55
Flewitt et al. 40, 41, 41–2
flooding metaphor 78
free-flow play 16, 37, 59
  affective alignment 25–6
free-flowing environments 59
free play 51, 52
functional extended self 121

games industry 106–8
gaming 68–9
gender 113
Gibson, J.J. 14–15
good parents identity 128–9, 148
Greenfield, Susan 103, 109
Gronn et al. 132–3
group identity 114
guerilla design approach 140, 145–7
guided interaction 17

Head Up Games (HUG) 56
heads up interaction 60
Hitron et al. 56–7
Hughes, Bob 52, 55, 55–6, 63, 79
human-computer-interaction design principles 56
hyper attention 103
hyperlinked texts 99

identity
  emerging sense of 114
  good parents 128–9, 148
  group identity 114
imagination 4–5, 66–7
  case study 67
  possibility thinking 68–73, 80
  ready-made materials 73–7, 80
  transgressive digital play 77–80
  see also creativity
immersion 69
independent games industry 106–8
  research 106–7
information processing, shallower 98, 99, 108
inner world 74
innovation 69
instincts 55
intangibility 39–41
Interactive Whiteboard (IWB) 13–14, 16, 126
  affordances of 15
  as an independent activity 136
  research 135–6
  sand-timer clue 59, 126, 136
intermediation 127, 128, 137
internet
  and cognitive changes 98–9
  as a risky place 128–9
iPads 40, 41
  availability during break times 61–2
  collaborative drawing 67
  research 41–2

jumping 35

Kelly, C. 29–30
Kids Doodle (app) 39, 70
kinderculture 84–5, 94
  Baby Shark (music video) 85
Kinect 35, 36
Kucirkova, N. & Sakr, M. 71–2

LEGO 90
literacy, children's 21, 22
literacy playshop 41
Lumino City (video game) 68–9, 92, 106
  case study 105

Madden (video game) 93
Magnusson, L.O. 116
makerspaces 41, 132
maladaptive cognitive shifts 97, 98, 103, 108
Marsh et al. 78–9
Marsh, J. 89–90
Marsh, J.A. 45–6
mash-up 74, 75
meddling in the middle 70
media literacy 83–4
  advertising 88
  case studies 84, 88
  commercialisation of childhood 88–91
  digital media and kinderculture 84–5, 94
  and parental mediation 91–3, 95
  research 86–7, 92–3
  screen time 92–3
media multitasking behaviour 99, 101
media, representation of digital play 129–30
medial literacy skills 92
mediation 94, 126–30, 137
  intermediation 127, 128
  lack of, adults 126
  and media literacy 91–3
  research 91
messy digital play 43–7, 48
  case study 43–4
Middlesex University 58
Mind Change (Greenfield) 103
Minecraft (video game) 106
Misslisibell 89, 95
moments of meeting 25–6
mouse, the (computer) 20–1
Mr Glue (app) 112
multi-tasking 103
multi-tasking behaviors 99
  research 101
music 84–5
music videos 84–5

narcissism 117, 119, 123
natural user interfaces 77
nature play 52
  case study 56–7
  and technology 55–7
needs of children 55, 147–9
non-digital environments
  creative play 73–4
  ready-made materials 73–4, 80
non-digital technologies 56, 58

online vlogs 115–16
ontological extended self 121
open questions 1–3, 4
originary technicity 55, 63

Our Story (app) 123
outdoor play 35, 36–7, 50–1
   barriers to 52
      social and material constraints 59–60
   case studies 51, 54, 56–7, 58–9
   decline in 51, 63, 141, 142
      and digital technologies 51–4
   parent-supervised 53–4
   personal impressions 60–1
   physical boundaries 59
   research 53–4
   safety and security 51, 52
   technology and nature play 55–7
   walking in the dark 54

parental mediation 91–3, 94, 95
parents
   good parents identity 128–9, 148
   lack of confidence in digital capabilities 126–7
   lack of proactive mediation 126–7
   reactive supervision 126
Pedersen, I. & Aspevig, K. 86–7
personalised story-making 112
photography 116–17, 118
   see also digital photography
physical activity 35, 46
physical engagement and sensory experience 34–5
   active digital play 35–8
   case study 35
   messy digital play 43–7
   and touch 39–42, 48
physical environment 44–5
physical properties 14, 15, 16
play instincts 52
playfulness 69
playshops 22, 44
Plowman et al. 16–17
Pokemon Go 36–7
possibility thinking 68–73, 80, 144–5
   case study 73
   features of 68, 69, 72, 80
   pedagogic strategies 69–70, 72, 80
   research 71–2
post-digital games 106, 109
proactive mediation 126–7
profiling learner agency 69–70
props 56–7
proximal guided interaction 17
psychological research 98
psychopathological disorders 35, 51
Puppet Pals (app) 21–2

Quest Atlantic (video game) 113
question-posing 69

RA et al. 104–5
rainy weather 52
reactive mediation 126–7
reactive supervision 126, 137
ready-made materials 73–7, 80
   case study 76–7
   digital remix 75
   research 75–6
real play 16, 31
remix 74–5
research
   ADHD (attention deficit hyperactivity disorder) 104–5
   collaborative creativity 21–2
   connected play 45–7
   connectedness 29–30
   digital cameras and three-year-olds 116–17
   digital disconnect 132–3
   digital photography 37–8
   digital technology at home and preschool 17
   emerging sense of identity 114
   human self 120–1
   independent games industry 106–7
   Interactive Whiteboard (IWB) 135–6
   iPads 41–2
      availability during break times 61–2
   mediation 91
   multi-tasking behaviors 101
   outdoors play 53–4
   possibility thinking 71–2
   ready-made materials 75–6
   screen time 92–3
   transgressive digital play 78–9
   unboxing videos 89–90
   vlogging 86–7
restrictive mediation 92, 94
risk-taking 69
rough and tumble play 68
rules 68

safety 51, 52
   parental mediation 91–3
Sakr, M. & Scollan, A. 135–6
Sarah and Duck (app) 1
scaffolding 30
scattered attention 100–2
Schilhab, T. 61–2
screen time 54, 92–3, 129, 130, 131, 144, 145
security 51, 52
self 111–12
   case studies 112, 118
   in relation to others 113–15, 122
      boys 113
      girls 113

self-presentation 111, 115–17, 122
self-representation 118–19, 122
selfies 119–21
selling of 87
and smartphones 119–21
self-conscious commodification 116
self-curating 118–19
self-determination 69
self-image 117
self-making 121
self-presentation 111, 115–17, 122
and selfies 119–21
self-representation 111, 118–19, 122
and selfies 119–21
selfies 43–4, 122
case study 118
self-presentation/self-representation 119–21
semiosis 75
sensory experience
loss of 132
see also physical engagement and sensory experience
sensory losses 132
Skype 29–30, 32
slowliness 40, 106, 109
smartphones 119–21
social interaction 12–13
affective alignment 25–6, 31
case study 13–14
collaborative creativity 19–22, 31, 39
connectedness vs. connection 28–30, 32
digital technologies in a sociocultural context 14–17
ocial media, child influencers 86–7
cial semiotic theory 15, 31
ciocultural context 14–17
ase study 18–19
iocultural theory 14–15
ary engagement 14, 15
ing, case study 134
fy (app) 102
gle (app) 39, 67
K. & Steinkuehler, C. 92–3
backstage 116
of selfhood 115
back 69
ursery schools 40
. 55, 63
ing 112

ie 70
rs 88
, 31

Tandon et al. 53–4
taxonomies of play 77, 78–9
technical mediation 91, 94
technicity 55
television, interaction with other digital devices 99, 101
threaded cognition 103
time and space 70
Toca Nature (app) 102
toddler crack 89
touch 39–42, 40, 48
drawing on an iPad 40, 41, 41–2
multimodal engagement 41
research 41–2
specific factors 40
transduction 45
transgressive digital play 77–80
research 78–9
transparent technology 56
turn-taking 15, 16, 126
Tux Paint 14, 18, 73

unboxing videos 88–9
research 89–90

vicarious pleasure 89, 90
vicarious touch 39, 41, 48
video games 68
emerging sense of identity 114
shared cultural reference point 114
videogaming 103
visual surplus 37
vlogging 86–7, 94–5, 115–16, 134

wallowing 28, 32
we-paradigm 19
web-mapping 127
websites 131
aimed at children 128–9
commercial 131
as learning environments 129
marketed as safe 128–9, 131
as a risky place 128–9, 131
what if thinking 68
WhatsApp 115
White, E.J. 37–8
Wii 35
Willett, R.J. 128–9
Wilson, D. 106
Wohlwend, K.E. 21–2

YouTube 44, 87, 134
unboxing videos 88–9
research 89–90